Frostiana

# Frostiana

## Or a History of the River Thames in a Frozen State

Edited by B. A. Thurber

———————————

Skating History Press

ISBN: 978-1-948100-02-1
LCCN: 2018940901


Skating History Press
Evanston, IL
http://www.skatinghistorypress.com/

# Contents

**Introduction**                                   **1**

Frost fairs                                          **3**

Printed on the Thames                              **15**

This edition                                       **19**

Bibliography                                       **21**


**Frostiana**                                      **25**

Advertisement                                      **29**

Introduction; containing an account of the
    late frost                  **31**
    Accounts from the country . . . . . . . . . . .   40
    Accidents  . . . . . . . . . . . . . . . . . . .   47

**Chapter I. Frost**                               **49**
    Freezing . . . . . . . . . . . . . . . . . . . . .   50
        Wonderful expansion of water in the act
            of freezing . . . . . . . . . . . . .   51
    Thames frozen 1715–16 . . . . . . . . . . . . .   53
    Thames frozen 1739–40 . . . . . . . . . . . . .   56
    Frost of 1767–68  . . . . . . . . . . . . . . . .   59
    Thames frozen 1788–89 . . . . . . . . . . . . .   60

Thames frozen 1814 . . . . . . . . . . . . .    63

Freezing rain, or raining ice . . . . . . . . .    71

Influence of frost on health . . . . . . . . . .    72

Frozen market at St. Petersburgh . . . . . . .    74

Chronological table of remarkable frosts through-
    out Europe . . . . . . . . . . . . . . . . .    75

## Chapter II. Snow                                 79

Uses of snow . . . . . . . . . . . . . . . . . .    83

Artificial snow . . . . . . . . . . . . . . . . . .    86

Snow slips . . . . . . . . . . . . . . . . . . . .    86

Account of a woman buried in the snow for
    eight days . . . . . . . . . . . . . . . . . .    87

The hot bath and snow-bath . . . . . . . . . .    90

Thomson's description of a man lost in the snow    93

## Chapter III. Ice                                 97

Ice-hills . . . . . . . . . . . . . . . . . . . . .    98

Icebergs . . . . . . . . . . . . . . . . . . . . .    99

Ice islands . . . . . . . . . . . . . . . . . . . .   102

Blink of the ice . . . . . . . . . . . . . . . . .   104

Union of sugar and ice by the agency of fire  .   106

Glaciers . . . . . . . . . . . . . . . . . . . . . .   108

An icy epitaph . . . . . . . . . . . . . . . . . .   112

How to make ice . . . . . . . . . . . . . . . . .   112

How to make ice cream . . . . . . . . . . . . .   114

A palace built of ice . . . . . . . . . . . . . .   115

Hamburgh ice-boat . . . . . . . . . . . . . . .   116

To render assistance to persons in danger of
    drowning . . . . . . . . . . . . . . . . . . .   119

To recover persons apparently drowned, as rec-
    ommended by the Humane Society  . . .   120

Construction of an ice-house . . . . . . . . . . 120
Morse-catching on the ice  . . . . . . . . . . 122

## Chapter IV. Cold                                    127

Natural history of cold . . . . . . . . . . . . 127
Effects of cold on the human frame . . . . . . 129
Effect of cold on vegetation  . . . . . . . . . 129
Singular effect of cold in Lapland . . . . . . . 130
Extreme cold of Siberia . . . . . . . . . . . . 131
Curious effect of cold on the feathered tribe  . 132
Miscellaneous effects of cold in foreign coun-
    tries, in former times . . . . . . . . . . . 133

## Chapter V. Northern winters                         135

A winter in Stockholm . . . . . . . . . . . . 136
Preparations for winter in Russia . . . . . . . 139
Virgil's description of a Scythian winter  . . . 140
Curious description of a Russian winter in 1603 143
Beautiful description of a winter at Copenhagen 145
The single night of Spitzbergen  . . . . . . . 147
Sledges . . . . . . . . . . . . . . . . . . . . 151
    Dutch sledges  . . . . . . . . . . . . . . 152
    Ship-sledges  . . . . . . . . . . . . . . . 153
    Lapland sledges . . . . . . . . . . . . . . 154
    Sledges in Kamschatka . . . . . . . . . . . 155

## Chapter VI. Skating                                 157

Origin of skating  . . . . . . . . . . . . . . 159
Rules for learners . . . . . . . . . . . . . . . 160

# List of Figures

1   The area of London in which frost fairs
    were held. The bridges across the river
    are Westminster, Blackfriars, and Lon-
    don (from left to right). Excerpt from
    Edward Mogg's "London in Miniature"
    (1806) courtesy of Wikimedia Commons
    with modifications by the editor.  . . . .   4
2   Title page of *The Great Frost*, STC 11403,
    Houghton Library, Harvard University.
    Courtesy of Wikimedia Commons. . . . .   7
3   The frost fair of 1683–84. From Andrews
    (1887:16–17) courtesy of Wikimedia Com-
    mons.  . . . . . . . . . . . . . . . . . .   8

4   The original title page of *Frostiana*. Ba-
    sed on the editor's photograph of the
    copy in the Newberry Library, Chicago. .  27

5   The ice-boat described by Günther. Top:
    Pushing it along the ice. Middle: Carry-
    ing it over uneven areas. Bottom: The
    bottom. Digitized by Google Books. . . .  118

6   The cart and cask Acerbi saw in Stock-
    holm. Digitized by Google Books. . . . .  137

# Introduction

# Frost fairs

In the past, frost fairs were held in London when the River Thames froze during cold, hard winters. These were rare and exciting events that got people outdoors despite the cold weather. They played games and skated on the ice. Booths were set up to sell food and commemorative merchandise. Schneer (2005:80) describes frost fairs as "abbreviated, focused versions of the larger society, but with a democratic twist" because people of all social classes played together on the ice. These fairs were held upstream of London Bridge in the area shown in figure 1. This area is called "above Bridge"; the other (downstream) side of London Bridge is called "below Bridge."

The Thames did not freeze hard enough for a fair to be held every year, or even every few years, which made frost fairs rare and exciting events. It is not clear when this tradition began; on page 75, *Frostiana* mentions booths built on the frozen Thames in 695. I have been unable to find evidence corroborating this statement, but, true or not, it shows that people thought the history of frost fairs went back that far. Frost fairs definitely go back to at least the seventeenth century and probably to the sixteenth. Schneer (2005:72) reports that nine frost fairs were held between 1564 and 1814, inclusive. All these fairs are described in nineteenth-century publications. *Frostiana* describes the frosts that were suitable for fairs during the eighteenth century (1715–16, 1739–40, 1767–68, and 1788–

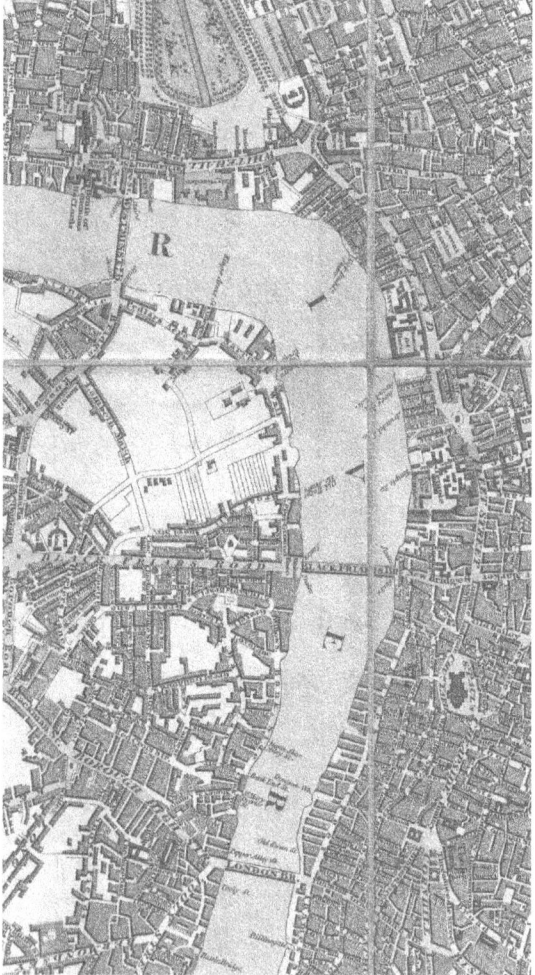

Figure 1: The area of London in which frost fairs were held. The bridges across the river are Westminster, Blackfriars, and London (from left to right). Excerpt from Edward Mogg's "London in Miniature" (1806) courtesy of Wikimedia Commons with modifications by the editor.

89—see pages 53–62) and, of course, the frost of 1813–
14. Walford (1887:34–40) reports frost fairs being held
in all these years except 1767–68. That accounts for
four of the nine fairs mentioned by Schneer. The others were held in the previous two centuries; Walford
(1887:17, 19–23, 25–33) describes additional frost fairs
held in 1564–65, 1607–08, 1620–21, 1683–84, and 1687–
88, but *Frostiana* skips over these.

The first frost fair may have been in 1564–65, but it
is not documented well. Schneer (2005:72) reports that
"boys played football in the middle of the frozen stream
and Queen Elizabeth, attended by her lords and ladies,
went frequently upon it to 'shoot at marks.'" Raphael
Holinshed (d. c. 1580) provides a contemporary and
rather more detailed description:

> The one and twentieth of December [1564]
> began a frost, which continued so extrem-
> lie, that on New yeares euen, people went
> ouer and alongst the Thames on the ise from
> London bridge to Westminster. Some plaied
> at the football as boldlie there, as if it had
> beene on the drie land: diuerse of the court
> being then at Westminster, shot dailie at
> pricks set vpon the Thames: and the people
> both men and women went on the Thames
> in greater numbers, than in anie stréet of
> the citie of London. On the third daie of
> Ianuarie at night it began to thaw, and on
> the fifth daie was no ise to be seene be-
> twéene London bridge and Lambeth, which
> sudden thaw caused great floods and high

waves, that bare downe bridges and houses, and drowned manie people in England: especiallie in Yorkshire, Owes bridge was borne awaie with others.

(Holinshed, 1808:IV.228)

This frost fair seems to have been a minor event in comparison with the ones to come. The next frost fair, in 1608–09, was documented more thoroughly in the commemorative book *The Great Frost*, whose title page is shown in figure 2. The third seventeenth-century frost fair, held in 1683–84 and shown in figure 3, earned a lasting reputation because it was held during the winter that went down in history as the coldest ever; even a century and a half later, ballads commemorating it were compiled (Rimbault, 1844). This frost fair was the best-documented of all, thanks in part to John Evelyn. In his diary entry for 24 January 1684, Evelyn describes the frost fair in detail:

The frost still continuing more & more severe, the Thames before London was planted with bothes in formal streetes, as in a Citty, or Continual faire, all sorts of Trades & shops furnished, & full of Commodities, even to a Printing presse, where the People & Ladys tooke a fansy to have their names Printed & the day & yeare set downe, when printed on the *Thames*: This humour tooke so universaly, that 'twas estimated the Printer gained five pound a day, for printing a line onely, at six-pence a Name, besides

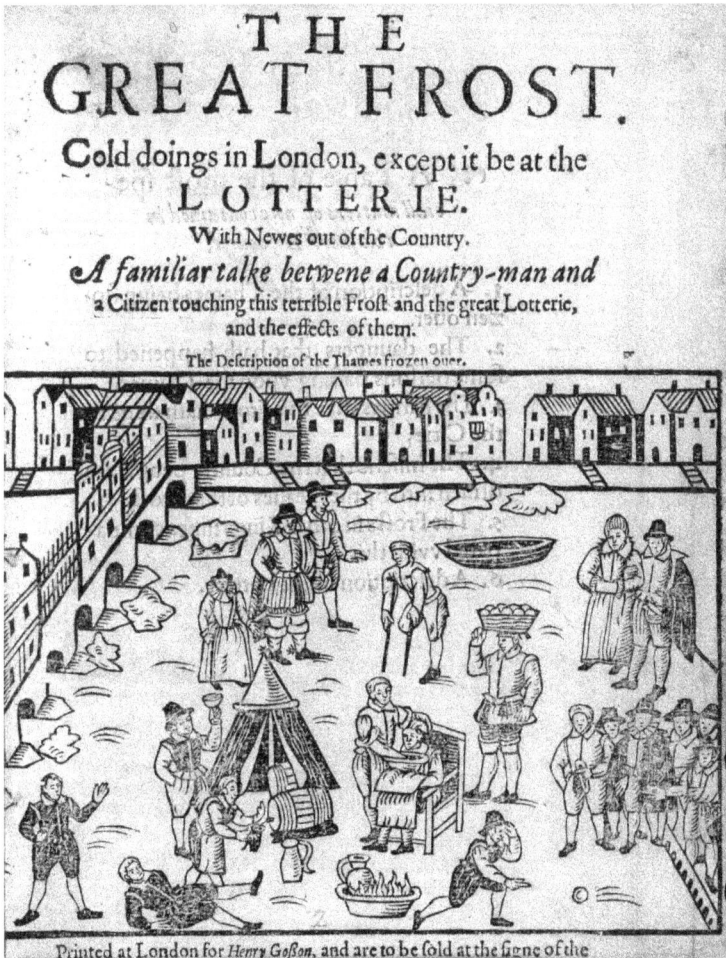

Figure 2: Title page of *The Great Frost*, STC 11403, Houghton Library, Harvard University. Courtesy of Wikimedia Commons.

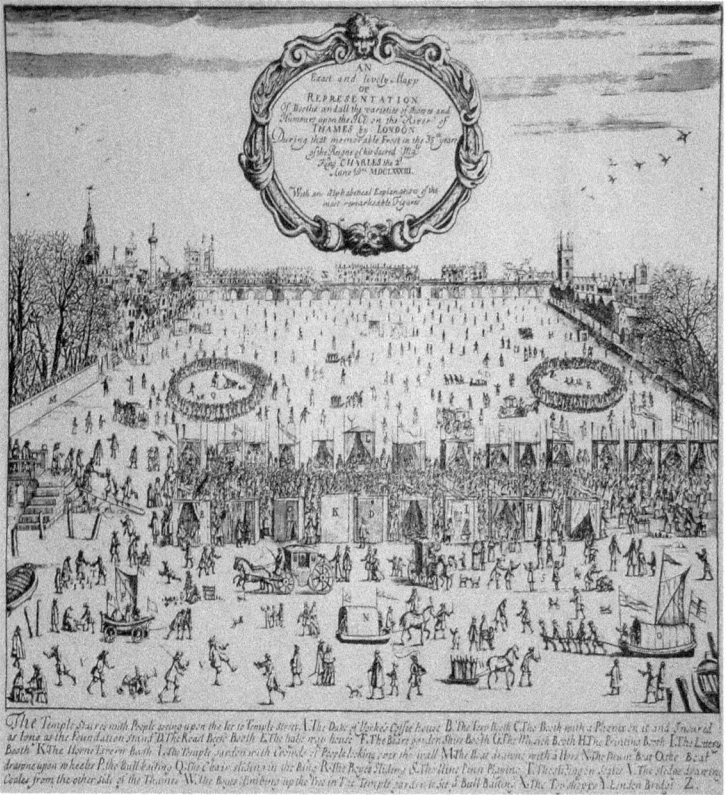

Figure 3: The frost fair of 1683–84. From Andrews (1887:16–17) courtesy of Wikimedia Commons.

what he gott by Ballads &c: Coaches now
plied from Westminster to the Temple, &
from severall other staires too & froo, as
in the streets; also on sleds, sliding with
skeetes; There was likewise Bull-baiting, Horse & Coach races, Pupet-plays & interludes,
Cookes & Tipling, & lewder places; so as
it seem'd to be a bacchanalia, Triumph or
Carnoval on the Water, whilst it was a severe Judgement upon the Land: the Trees
not onely splitting as if lightning-struck, but
Men & Cattell perishing in divers places,
and the very seas so locked up with yce,
that no vessells could stirr out, or come in.
(de Beer, 1955:IV.361–362)

This frost fair was called a "Blanket Fair," as Walford
(1887:31–32) notes, "in consequence of the booths being largely formed of blankets, which, like 'Goldsmith's
chest of drawers, did double duty,' as we learn from a
doggerel broadside:—

Like Babel, this fair's not built with brick
    or stone
Though here, I believe, is great confusion
New blankets are forced a double duty to
    pay
As beds all the night, and for houses all
    day."

The other seventeenth-century frost fairs are less well-
documented. The eighteenth-century fairs are described

in *Frostiana*, which appears to have been used by both Andrews (1887) and Walford (1887) as they put together their descriptions.

In addition to the frost fairs, both Andrews and Walford, like the compiler of *Frostiana*, describe other years that featured hard frosts without mentioning frost fairs, which implies that frost fairs may not have been held every year that was sufficiently cold—extremely cold weather was a necessary but not sufficient condition for a frost fair. Other factors, whether social, economic, or meteorological, were also involved. Those factors aligned for the last time in the winter of 1813–14, when the last frost fair on the Thames was held.

It is unlikely that this frost fair will lose the distinction of being last, not because of climate change, but because of changes in the Thames. The river froze in the past because the old London Bridge had many closely-spaced supports. During winter, ice would jam against them, stopping the river's flow. This led to a large pool of stagnant water just above the bridge, which froze relatively easily. In 1825, work on a replacement bridge began (Lockwood et al., 2017:22), and in 1831, London Bridge was replaced (Schneer, 2005:70). In subsequent years, embankments were built. These changes made the river flow faster, which significantly decreased its likelihood of freezing (Lockwood et al., 2017:22).

*Frostiana* commemorates the last frost fair and is among the most important sources of information on frost fairs; Andrews (1887), for example, reports having consulted "several hundred books, magazines, and newspapers" in addition to having "derived much valuable information from a scarce book printed on the Ice of the River Thames, in the year 1814, and published under the title of 'Frostiana.'" It is likely that *Frostiana* drew on a similarly long list of sources, many of which are now lost. It is not clear who actually did the work of assembling *Frostiana*. The best candidate for overseeing the work George Davis, the publisher, who is sometimes listed as the author. He may have instructed one of his apprentices or other employees to compile the material.

Much of the introduction and six chapters that make up *Frostiana* is devoted to recounting tales of great frosts and their consequences for people. These are intermixed with ideas about the science behind freezing and clever explanations of useful skills, such as rescuing drowning people and making ice cream. The final chapter of *Frostiana*, "Skating," provides some insight into the development of figure skating.

Skating had been known in England for some time; John Evelyn's diary entry (quoted above) shows that skating ("sliding with skeetes") was also part of the 1683–84 frost fair. However, despite its popularity and already long history, figure skating seems to have still been in its infancy in 1814. The emphasis of the chapter in *Frostiana* is on skating as "an amusement" and the cultivation of "elegant and graceful attitudes" (p. 162) rather than the technical requirements of compulsory figures, which came later. Inside and outside edges were known, but skaters were advised to put lead shot

in their skating-side pockets to help them get onto their
outside edges (page 161). Some 83 years later, G. Herbert Fowler commented on the absurdity of this advice:

> the literature of 1800 to 1820 seems to in-
> dicate that the art [skating] had gone back-
> ward rather than forward. It is about this
> period that one frequently meets the sug-
> gestion that the outside edge should be lear-
> nt by placing a bag of lead shot in the pocket
> of the side to which one is to lean; and one
> book, which devotes a chapter to the Art of
> Skating, gives also directions "How to make
> Ice Cream!" (Thurber, 2018:56)

*Frostiana* is that book; the instructions for making ice
cream can be found on page 114.

The idea of skating on the Thames during the frost
fair has become so popular that it made its way into
Doctor Who: in series 6, episode 7, River mentions that
the Doctor took her skating at the 1814 frost fair for
her birthday. This fair was also the setting of Doctor Who series 10, episode 3 ("Thin Ice"), which featured an elephant crossing the Thames, an event that
has gone down in popular history as something remarkable. It was first noted in newspapers of the time; on
5 February 1814, the *Ipswich Journal* reported that on
"Wednesday [2 February] a very fine Elephant crossed
the Thames a little below Blackfriar's Bridge; the sin-
gularity of such an animal on the ice attracted a great
concourse of spectators." This elephant may have been
the "admired and wonderfully docile and sagacious" elephant that was "exhibited, richly ornamented, attended

by his Keeper, Children, &c" described in *The Times* a few days later. This spectacle is not mentioned in *Frostiana*, but it seems reasonable to suppose that the elephant did in fact cross the river, since there is evidence corroborating its presence in London.

Today, just over two centuries later, *Frostiana* continues to inspire readers with its stories and advice. Its wide range of topics makes it interesting to historians of ice skating and of London as well as climate scientists. *Frostiana* continues to commemorate last frost fair and the tradition of frost fairs on the Thames.

# Printed on the Thames

The title page of *Frostiana* includes the impressive claim that it was "Printed and published on the ICE on the River *Thames, February 5, 1814*, by G. DAVIS." This seems to imply that the entire book was printed on the Thames, but a careful reading of the text shows that this was not the case. The end of the advertisement (page 30) backs off from this grandiose claim by clarifying that only the title page was actually printed on the Thames:

> *As an additional object of* curiosity, *it may be proper to mention, that a large impression of the* Title *page of this work, was* actually printed *on the* ICE *on the* RIVER THAMES!!

This restricted claim seems more reasonable.

I examined the copy at the Newberry Library in Chicago to determine whether "title page" refers to only the title page or to the first quire (as proposed by Kane (2014)). I found that the codicological evidence supports the literal truth of the statement in the advertisement: only the single title page was been printed on the ice. This section explains why.

*Frostiana*'s small pages[1] are portions of large sheets of paper that were printed on both sides and then folded into quires. The quires were sewn together in the binding. *Frostiana* has 12 pages in each quire, but there

---

[1]The pages measure approximately $7\frac{3}{8}$ by $4\frac{3}{8}$ inches.

is a bit of weirdness in the front of the book, which is
the part that is important here. The front matter is as
follows:

- Blank sheet (endpaper)

- Title page (pages i–ii)

- Advertisement (pages iii–iv)

- Table of contents (pages v–vi)

- Introduction (pages viii–xxii)

- Chapter I (starting on page 1 or xxiii)

Stitching shows between pages viii and ix, which
means this is the center of a quire. Page xv has a "c"
centered at the bottom, which marks it as the first page
of a new quire. This means that pages ix through xiv
comprise the second part of a full quire. These six pages
must match up with the first six pages, i.e., pages iii–
viii. Further evidence for this is the "b" at the bottom
of the Advertisement and the "b3" at the bottom of the
first page of the Introduction. Throughout the book,
the beginning of each new quire is labeled with a letter,
and the fifth page is labeled with that letter plus the
number "3."

The outcome of this is that the title page (pages
i–ii) is not part of any quire! I examined the binding
as carefully as I could without distressing the reading
room attendant, and it looked like it was glued in between the front endpaper and the first page of the Advertisement very carefully—but not carefully enough.

Whoever bound this particular copy of *Frostiana* made a telling mistake: the lower right corner of the back of the title page is folded up instead of being firmly attached to the binding. It is also noteworthy that the title page is slightly shorter than the endpaper and the first page of the Advertisement. This means that the "additional object of curiosity" mentioned at the end of the Advertisement should be taken literally. Only the title page, which is small and single-sided, was printed on the ice. In fact, internal evidence shows that the text of the book was not even complete by the time the ice broke up. Page 71 includes the statement that

> While we are now writing, (half past 2 p. m. [on Feb. 7]) *a printing press has been again set up on a large* ICE-ISLAND, between Blackfriars and Westminster-bridges. At this *new printing-office*, the remainder of a large impression of the *Title-page* of the present work is now actually being printed, so that the purchasers of FROSTIANA, will have this additional advantage.

Although this brings to mind the image of young printers frantically slaving away over a printing press in the face of impending doom in the form of a trip to the bottom of an extremely cold river, it makes the printer's undertaking seem rather less heroic than printing the entire book on the ice. Instead of hauling a large, heavy printing press to the ice, a very small one would have sufficed. Alternatively, a full sheet of the title page could have been printed and individual title pages cut out and sold. Waiting for the pages to dry to print on the back would have been unnecessary. The work would have gone relatively quickly, making a large print run possible. People could have bought the title page on the ice and brought it to the printer's shop to be bound into the finished book later or purchased the complete book after the frost fair had ended.

*Frostiana* was not George Davis's only foray into printing on the ice during the frost fair. The Cambridge University Library holds a small piece of paper with the words "Printed on the River Thames, Feb. 3, 1814." in print that looks "identical to that used for the title page of *Frostiana*" (Sims, 2013). It seems that Mr. Davis (and, presumably, his employees and apprentices) spent the fair diligently working a press on the ice. They followed in a long tradition of printing small collectibles on the ice to commemorate frost fairs; many such pieces of ephemera—with the inscriptions repeated in the pages of *Frostiana*—can be found in special collections and archives in the United Kingdom.

# This edition

This edition of *Frostiana* is based on the scanned pdf version made available by the National Oceanic and Atmospheric Administration and the physical copy at the Newberry Library in Chicago. I have left the spelling and punctuation as they are in the original, except for correcting obvious errors and adjusting the capitalization of section headings. I also followed the original in the use of fonts, except that I have not begun sections in small caps. All footnotes are my own unless otherwise noted; the illustrations are also my additions. I have traced some of the compiler's sources and have placed footnotes throughout the text accordingly.

# Bibliography

Andrews, W.
  1887. *Famous Frosts and Frost Fairs in Great Britain: Chronicled from the Earliest to the Present Time.* London: George Redway.

Anonymous
  18 March 2014. A moment in London's history—when the last 'frost fair' was held on the Thames. *Exploring London.* http://exploring-london.com.

Anonymous
  1871. Skating. In *Beeton's Historical Romances, Daring Deeds, and Animal Stories*, S. O. Beeton, ed., pp. 102–107. London: Ward, Lock, and Tyler.

Anonymous
  31 March 2018. Ice-skating speed record broken in Luleå, Sweden. *The Local.* https://www.thelocal.se/.

Anonymous
  5 February 1814a. Friday's post. *Ipswich Journal.*

Anonymous
  8 February 1814b. The times. *Times (London)*, p. 2.

Chang, H.
  2004. *Inventing Temperature: Measurement and Scientific Progress.* Oxford: Oxford University Press.

de Beer, E. S., ed.
    1955. *The Diary of John Evelyn*. Oxford: Clarendon
    Press.

Holinshed, R.
    1808. *Chronicles of England, Scotland, and Ireland*.
    London: J. Johnson; F. C. and J. Rivington; T.
    Payne; Wilkie and Robinson; Longman, Hurst, Bees,
    and Orme; Cadell and Davies; and J. Mawman.

Hunter, M. and E. B. Davis, eds.
    1999. *The Works of Robert Boyle*. London: Pickering
    and Chatto, Limited.

International Skating Union
    11 December 2017. Bloemen (CAN) wraps up week-
    end with epic 5000m world record. *WC Speed Skating
    News*. https://isu.org/news/.

Kane, K.
    7 March 2014. *Frostiana* by George Davis. *The Re-
    gency Redingote*.
    https://regencyredingote.wordpress.com/.

Küchelmann, H. C. and P. Zidarov
    2005. Let's skate together! Skating on bones in the
    past and today. In *From Hooves to Horns, from Mol-
    lusc to Mammoth: Manufacture and Use of Bone
    Artefacts from Prehistoric Times to the Present,
    Proceedings of the 4th Meeting of the ICAZ Worked
    Bone Research Group at Tallinn, 26th–31st of August
    2003*, H. Luik, A. M. Choyke, C. Batey, and L. Löu-
    gas, eds., volume 15 of *Muinasaja Teadus*, pp. 425–
    445. Tallinn: Ajaloo Instituut.

Lockwood, M., M. Owens, E. Hawkins, G. S. Jones, and I. Usoskin
2017. Frost fairs, sunspots and the little ice age. *Astronomy and Geophysics*, 58(2):2.17–2.23. doi:10.1093/astrogeo/atx057.

Mills, A.
1870. *The Literature and the Literary Men of Great Britain and Ireland*. New York: Harper and Brothers.

OED
2018. Oxford English Dictionary Online. http://www.oed.com/.

Rimbault, E. F., ed.
1844. *Old Ballads Illustrating the Great Frost of 1683–4 and the Fair on the River Thames*. London: Percy Society.

Schneer, J.
2005. *The Thames*. New Haven: Yale University Press.

Sims, L.
9 April 2013. Printed 'Frost Fair' ephemera in the University Library. *Cambridge University Library Special Collections*. https://specialcollections-blog.lib.cam.ac.uk/.

Thurber, B. A., ed.
2018. *G. Herbert Fowler. On the Outside Edge: Being Diversions in the History of Skating*. Evanston, IL: Skating History Press.

Vandervell, H. E. and T. M. Witham
1869. *A System of Figure-Skating: Being the Theory and Practice of the Art as Developed in England, with a Glance at Its Origin and History*, first edition. London: Macmillan and Co.

Walford, E.
1887. *Frost Fairs on the Thames*, volume 12 of *Privately Printed Opuscula Issued to the Members of the Sette of Odd Volumes*. London: C. W. H. Wyman.

Whitelaw, J.
1805. *An Essay on the Population of Dublin: Being the Result of an Actual Survey Taken in 1798, with Great Care and Precision, and Arranged in a Manner Entirely New*. Dublin: Graisberry and Campbell.

# Frostiana

# FROSTIANA:

OR

A HISTORY OF

# THE RIVER THAMES,

In a Frozen State;

WITH AN ACCOUNT OF

## THE LATE SEVERE FROST;

AND THE WONDERFUL EFFECTS

OF

## Frost, Snow, Ice, and Cold,

IN ENGLAND,

AND IN DIFFERENT PARTS OF THE WORLD;

INTERSPERSED

WITH VARIOUS AMUSING ANECDOTES.

TO WHICH IS ADDED,

## THE ART OF SKATING.

A *dreadful winter* came; *each day* severe,
*Misty* when mild, and *icy-cold* when clear.
CRABBE.

## London:

Printed and published on the ICE on the River *Thames*,
*February* 5, 1814, by G. DAVIS,
Sold also by Sherwood, Neely, and Jones, Paternoster Row.

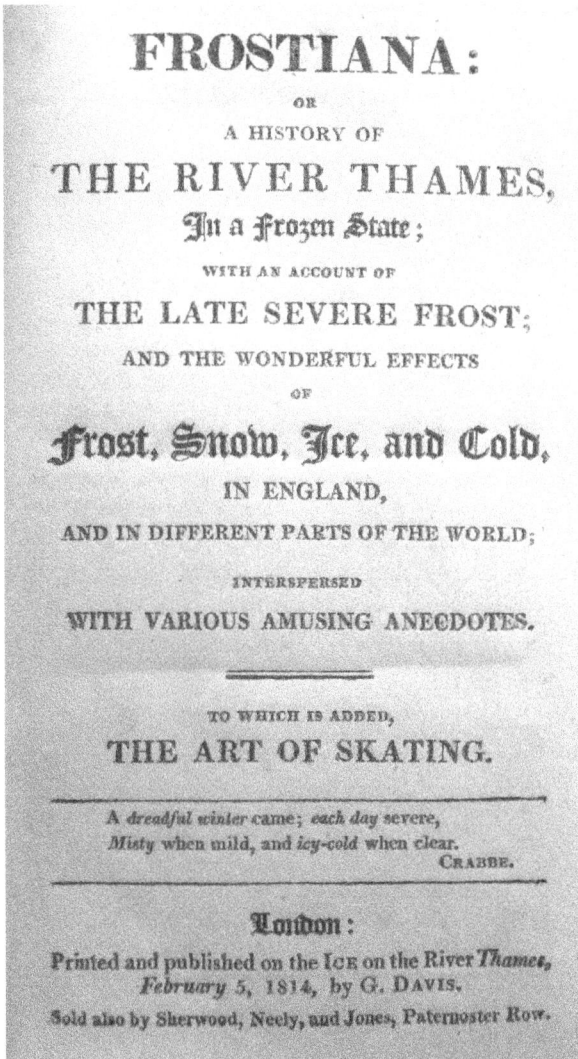

Figure 4: The original title page of *Frostiana*. Based on the editor's photograph of the copy in the Newberry Library, Chicago.

# Advertisement

O Winter! ruler of the inverted year,
Thy scattered hair, with sleet-like ashes filled,
Thy breath congealed upon thy lips, thy
    cheeks
Fringed with a beard made white with other
    snows
Than those of age; thy forehead wrapped in
    clouds,
A leafless branch thy sceptre, and thy throne
A sliding car, indebted to no wheels
But urged by storms along its slipp'ry way;
I love thee, all unlovely as thou seem'st,
And dreaded as thou art.       COWPER.[2]

*To the reflecting mind, nothing can be more agreeable than a philosophical account of the marvellous productions of* NATURE.*—This enables us to look through Nature up to* NATURE'S GOD, *and forms one of the most pleasing tasks:—whether the beauties of Spring, the lavish gifts of Summer; the rich fruits of Autumn; or the sterile grandeur of* WINTER, *be the object of our contemplation.*

*The attentive observer, as he walks forth to explore the dreary scenes around him, will find abundance of pleasure and instruction in the investigation of the various phenomena peculiar to this inclement season. The rigours of the present Winter indeed, are almost with-*

---

[2]From William Cowper, "The Task" (c. 1785), 4.120–129.

out a parallel in the annals af English Meteorology, and they accordingly, have excited more than ordinary notice.

To gratify, as well as to stimulate inquiry, we have not only given a philosophical explanation of Frost, Snow, Ice, and Cold, but have enlivened our descriptions by various anecdotes of their wonderful effects in England, and in different parts of the world.

An Introduction is prefixed, containing a full account of the late severe frost; and, in another part of the work, will be found an amusing narrative of the events which took place on the frozen surface of THAMES, from the 30th of January to the 5th of February inclusive.

As an additional object of curiosity, it may be proper to mention, that a large impression of the Title page of this work, was actually printed on the ICE on the RIVER THAMES!!

SNOW-HILL,
February 5th, 1814.

# Introduction; containing an account of the late frost

The late severe frost was ushered in by a *fog*, which for its density and duration has seldom been equalled. The winter of 1795 was marked by much the same circumstances as the present; the nights were so extremely foggy, that torches were used in the streets; coals were 4*s.* a bushel; and vegetables extremely dear. But, the only fog, at all comparable to that of 1813, was one which happened on the evening of new year's day, 1730, when many lives were lost in London in consequence. The fog was so dense that several persons fell into Fleet-ditch, and others into the Canal in St. James's Park, by mistaking their way; much damage was also done on the Thames.

The great fog which preceded the late frost, commenced, in London, on the evening of the 27th of December, 1813, about two hours before Lord Castlereagh set out from London on his way to embark for the continent. Happily his lordship proceeded on his journey, without interruption;—it was not so with the PRINCE REGENT, who, intending to pay a visit to the Marquis of Salisbury at Halfield House, was obliged to return back to Carlton House, after one of his outriders had fallen into a ditch on this side of Kentish Town, and which short excursion occupied several hours. Mr. Croker, of the Admiralty, also wishing to proceed on a visit northward, wandered in the dark, for several hours, without making more than three or four miles progress.

This tremendous fog, or 'darkness that might be *felt!* continued till the 3rd of January. On most of the roads, excepting the high north road, travelling was performed with the utmost danger, and the progress of the mails was greatly impeded. On Wednesday, the 29th, of December, the Birmingham mail was nearly *seven* hours in going from the Post-office to a mile or two below Uxbridge, a distance of 20 miles only: on this, and the other evenings, the short stages in the neighbourhood of London had two persons with links,[3] running by the horses' heads; nevertheless, with this, and other precautions, some serious, and many whimsical accidents occurred. Pedestrians even carried links or lanterns, and many, who were not provided with these illuminators, lost themselves in the most frequented, and at other times well known streets. Hackney-coachmen mistook the pathway for the road, and *vice versa,*—the greatest confusion occurring.

On the 31st of December, the state of the metropolis, in consequence of the increased fog, was, at night, truly alarming. It required great attention and knowledge of the public streets to proceed any distance, and those persons who had any material business to transact were unavoidably compelled to carry torches. The

---

[3]Torches "made of tow and pitch (?sometimes of wax or tallow), formerly much in use for lighting people along the streets"; this use goes back to the sixteenth century (OED, 2018:s.v. "link, n.[3]").

usual lamps appeared through the haze no bigger than small candles. The more careful hackney-coachmen got off the box and led their horses, while others drove only at a walking pace. There were frequent meetings of carriages, and great mischief ensued. Among the passengers much caution and apprehension prevailed. Many alarmed at the idea of being run down, made exclamations, such as "Who is coming?"—"Mind!"—"Take care!" &c. Females who had ventured abroad before the fog came on, were placed under great peril; several missed their way. Such was the extreme density of the atmosphere on Tuesday evening, the 28th, that the Maidenhead coach, on its return from town, missed the road near Harford Bridge, and was overturned. Lord Hawarden was among the passengers, and received an injury by the accident.

Almost immediately on the cessation of the fogs, heavy falls of snow took place. There is nothing in the memory of man to equal these falls. After several shorter intervals, the snow continued incessantly for 48 hours, and this too after the ground was covered with a condensation, the result of nearly four weeks continued frost. Almost the whole of the time the wind blew continually from the north and north-east, and was intensely cold. A short thaw also, which scarcely lasted one day, only rendered the state of the streets so much the worse. Hence the mass of snow and water became so thick, that it was with difficulty that hackney-coaches, with an additional horse, and other vehicles could plough their way through. Almost all kinds of trades and callings, carried on in the streets, stopped,

which considerably increased the distresses of the lower
orders. Few carriages, even stages, could travel on the
roads, which, even about town seemed deserted. From
many buildings, icicles, full a yard and a half long, were
seen suspended. The house water-pipes were all frozen,
whence it became necessary to have plugs in the streets
for the supply of all ranks of people. The Thames, from
London Bridge to Blackfriars, was for nearly a fortnight
completely blocked up at ebb tide.

All the ponds and rivers in the neighbourhood of
London were completely frozen, and skating was pursued with great avidity on the Canal in St. James's,
and the Serpentine in Hyde Park. On Monday, the 10th
of January, the Canal and the Basin in the Green Park
were conspicuous for the number of *steel-shod* heroes
who covered their glassy surfaces, and who, according
to their respective qualities, administered to the pleasure of the throng which crowded their banks; some by
the agility and grace with which they performed their
evolutions, and others by the tumbles and other accidents which marked their clumsy career. There was, as
usual, a motley collection of all orders of his Majesty's
subjects, engaged in the busy scene, who seemed all
alike eager candidates for the applause of the multitude, and whether *sweep, dustman, drummer,* or *beau,*
each seemed conscious of possessing some claim, not
only to his own good opinion, but to that of the fair
*belles* who viewed his movements. There were several
accidents in the course of the day, but none we believe
of a serious nature.

While these Parks were thus numerously attended,

Hyde Park had to boast of a more distinguished order of
visitors, who, in the course of the afternoon, flocked in
prodigious crowds to the banks of the Serpentine, which
was covered with most excellent ice. Notwithstanding
the keenness of the breeze, several females of dash, clad
in robes of the richest fur, bid defiance to its chilling
embrace, and, on the fragile bosom of the river ventured
their fair frames. The skaters were in great numbers,
and were of first-rate note. Some of the most difficult
movements of the art were executed with an agility and
grace which excited universal admiration.

A lady and two officers performed a reel with a precision scarcely conceivable, and attracted a very numerous circle of spectators, whose boisterous applause so
completely terrified the fair cause of their ecstasy, as
to induce her to forego the pleasure she herself received
from the amusement, and to put an end to that which
she afforded to such as were disposed to admire her in
silence.

Two unfortunate accidents, occurred; one *skating*
lady dislocated the *patella* or kneepan, and five gentlemen and a lady were immersed in the icy fluid, but
received no farther injury than a severe ducking.

On the 20th of January, in consequence of the great
accumulation of snow heaped upon the ground, it became necessary to relieve the roofs of the houses by
throwing off the load collected upon them; and by these
means the carriage-ways in the middle of the streets
were rendered scarcely passable for man or horse; and
all the conveniencies described in pp. 33, 34, were the
consequence. The streams constantly flowing from the

open plugs, added to the general mass of ice. An enormous increase took place in the price of coals, as the River navigation and other means of conveyance were entirely obstructed.

The continuation of the frost and snow induced many coach proprietors, particularly on the northern and western roads, not to continue running their coaches until a change of weather should take place. In many places where the road lies low, the snow had drifted higher than the coaches, which was the case as near town as Finchley Common. The snow had drifted into the road in the course of one night, a depth of sixteen feet, and it was impassable at first even to oxen. On Bagshot-heath there was a complete stoppage, and many accidents occurred by vehicles getting off the road. About Esher and Cobham again the road was completed choaked up.

With the exception of the Kent and Essex roads, no others were passable but a few miles out of London. The coaches on the western road remained stationary at different parts. The Windsor coach got through the snow at Colnbrook, which was sixteen feet deep, by employing about fifty labourers. Lower down, at Maidenhead-lane, the snow drifted to a great depth; and between Twyford and Reading it assumed quite a mountainous appearance. On parts of Bagshot-heath, it is impossible to convey an adequate idea of its situation. The Newcastle coach went off the road into a pit upwards of eight feet deep, but without doing mischief to either man or horse. The middle North-road was impassable as near as Highgate-hill.

On the 22d of January, and for some days afterwards, the ice on the Serpentine River exhibited a singular appearance, from the mountains of snow which
the sweepers had collected together in different situations. The spaces allotted for the skaters were in the
forms of circles, squares, and oblongs. Next to the carriage ride (on the north side) were many astonishing
evolutions displayed. Skipping on skates, and the Turk-
cap backwards,[4] were among the most conspicuous. A
sledge was drawn by a poney, *rough-shod.*[5] The ice was
not good, it being injured by the partial thaw in some
places, and in others much *cut up.*—It was highly amusing to see the most elegantly dressed females *dashing*
through the hillocks of snow.

Among the extraordinary aspects and appearances
of the late severe weather, the state of the river Thames
was not the least singular. Vast quantities of pieces of
floating ice, loaden generally with heaps of snow, were
seen almost every where on the surface; and being carried up and down by the tide or the stream, and collected where the projecting banks or the bridges made
a resistance to the flow, and a support to the accumulation, sometimes forming a chain of glaciers, united one
moment,—at another clashing and cracking and dashing in a singular and awful manner: again, when the
flood beneath was not sufficiently elevated to support
the mass, and when the current passed strongly, the

---

[4]The Turk's Cap "is nothing less than making a number of
semicircles like repeated threes on the same foot, for these describe the convolutions of a turban" (Anonymous, 1871:107).

[5]"Rough-shod" refers to the practice of adding small spikes
to horseshoes to give them traction while walking on ice.

ice islands floated away, clashing and cracking as they went, rising one over another, and then receding, covered with angry foam, as the violence of the wind or wave impelled them.

In passing through the arches of the bridges, the crash was tremendous: for near the bridges, the floating pieces collected about mid-water, or while the current was less forcible, and ranged themselves regularly one line upon another, the stream forming them into order as it passed, where it made its way in force, till the increasing confinement of the channel added such violence to the conflict, that a disruption took place, and the broken ice, with a crash, burst away again, and was carried up or down with the tide or the stream. The river was entirely frozen over for the space of a week, and a complete FROST FAIR held upon it, a circumstantial account of which will be found in Chapter I. FROST, page 49 and following pages.

Never since the establishment of mail coaches did correspondence meet with such general interruption as on this occasion. Internal communication was completely at a stand till the roads could be in some degree cleared; for besides the drifts by which they were rendered impassable, the whole face of the country presented one uniform sheet of snow, no trace of road being discoverable; and travellers had to make their path at the risk of being every moment overwhelmed. Waggons, carts, coaches, and vehicles of all descriptions, were left in the midst of the storm. The drivers finding they could proceed no farther, took the horses to the first convenient place, and there waited till a passage could be cut to enable them to proceed with safety.

Nothing could exceed the exertions of the Post-office in having the roads cleared in all directions for the conveyance of the mails, to and from the capital. The government also very properly interfered, and instructions were sent to every parish in the kingdom to employ labourers to clear the roads.

The snow accumulated in the midland counties, particularly on the borders of Northamptonshire and Warwickshire, to a height altogether unprecedented. In the neighbourhood of Dunchurch (a small village on the road to Birmingham, through Coventry), and for a few miles round that place, in all directions, the drifts exceeded the height of twenty-four feet, and no tracks of carriages or travellers could be discovered on the roads thereabouts, except on the great road, for many days.

The Cambridge mail-coach in coming to town, sunk into a hollow part of the road, and remained in that situation, with the snow drifting over it, from one o'clock to nine in the morning, when it was dragged out by fourteen waggon horses. Several passengers were in the coach the whole of the time; they were nearly frozen to death.

On Wednesday the 26th, the wind having veered round to the south-west, the effects of a thaw were speedily discernible. The fall of the river at London-bridge for some days presented a scene both novel and interesting. At the ebbing of the tide, huge fragments of ice were precipitated down the stream with great violence, accompanied by a noise, equal to the report of a small piece of artillery. On the return of the tide, they were forced back again; but the obstacles opposed to their passage through the arches were so great, as apparently to threaten a total stoppage to the navigation of the river at this essential point, and which probably would have soon taken place had the frost continued with unabated severity.

On Thursday, Friday, and Saturday, the 27th, 28th, and 29th, the thaw continued, and the roads and streets were nearly impassable from floods, and the accumulation of snow. But on Sunday the 30th a sharp frost set in, and continued till the next Saturday evening, the 5th of February.

## Accounts from the country

These narratives respecting the heavy falls of snow are truly astonishing; we select some of the most remarkable.

*Falmouth.* The weather has been more severe in this county, than has been remembered for twenty years. Heavy falls of snow, succeeded by hard frosts, have rendered all travelling by coach impracticable, and even on horseback highly dangerous. The mail coach, which started from this town for Exeter was overturned after having proceeded a few miles, but happily no material injury was sustained, by either passengers, driver, or guard. With much difficulty the coach was enabled, with the assistance of an additional pair of horses to reach the first stage; after which all endeavours to go farther were found perfectly useless. The letters were, however, sent to Bodmin by the guard on horseback. The Falmouth and Plymouth coach has been prevented from travelling by the snow, and the passengers have been obliged to remain at St. Austell. We have no doubt that, farther to the eastward, the roads are in a still worse condition, as our last Plymouth letters mention, that the snow was then nearly four feet high in several of the streets in that town, and that all coaches for Exeter, &c. are unable to travel.

*Liverpool, Jan. 17.* We have now had three weeks of the most rigorous frost which has been remembered for a great number of years. Fahrenheit's thermometer stood at 15 degrees (17 below the freezing point,) at the Athenæum; in the country it was no doubt much lower. Such a quantity of ice has been accumulated in the Mersey, that boats could not pass over. Almost every kind of labour performed without doors is nearly at a stand.

*Gloucester, Jan. 17.* The severity of the frost, for the last fortnight, has not been exceeded by any that has preceded it. The Severn is frozen over, and the ice is "in many places" sufficiently strong to sustain persons on its surface: indeed, several people going to Tewkesbury market on Wednesday last, rode across the ice on horseback, at the Lode, near that place.

On Monday the cold was so intense, that the thermometer, exposed in a north-eastern aspect, stood at

13 degrees, which is 9 below the freezing point.[6]  On
the eastern coast, it stood as low as 9 and 10; a degree
of cold very unusual in this county.

*Bristol, Jan. 18.* The frost continues in this city
with unusual severity. Our Floating Harbour now exhibits quite a novel scene: from Cumberland Basin to
the Feeder, at the bottom of Avon-street, it is one continued sheet of ice; and for the first time in the memory
of man, the skater made his appearance under Bristol
Bridge. The river Severn also is frozen over at various
points, so as to bear the weight of passengers.

*Whitehaven, Jan. 18.* The frost which seemed likely
to continue, has increased in severity, and is at this time
more intense than ever. All the ponds, streams, &c. in
this neighbourhood, are frozen; and there is scarcely a
pump in this town that is not dry. The observations
as to the thermometer are various; but all agree in as-
certaining these instruments to be considerably lower
than they have been for many years past.

The snow, which fell in great quantities on the night
of Sunday the 9th, has been increased in a very considerable degree, by repeated heavy showers, and the
whole rendered particularly severe by the high winds
which prevailed during the earlier part of the storm,
drifting the snow in many situations in such a manner,
as to make travelling very tedious as well as dangerous,
and in some places entirely blocking up the roads.

The effect has been to render the arrival of the post
and carriers very uncertain. The former have for a week

---

[6]There is a math error here; 13 degrees is 19 below freezing,
not 9.

past been several hours later than the usual time. Our market, on Wednesday, was very thinly attended, it having been found (in many parts) impossible to travel until the snow was cut.

We understand the snow laid the deepest between Wigton and Cockermouth. A few miles to the south of this town there was little in comparison; but a great deal fell on Sunday last: and we hear that towards the evening it was nearly three feet deep on the road between Whitehaven and Egremont.

*Dublin, Jan. 14.* It is supposed that the present fall of snow has been as heavy as any ever known in Ireland. But as to the quantity, there seems to be no doubt of its being greater than ever before experienced in the same space of time. In this respect, we can answer that it is unparalleled for half a century, upon the authority of a very intelligent gentleman in this city, who has kept a regular diary of the weather for the last 50 years. The snow preceding Monday was so slight, as hardly to occasion even a remark, and yet, in the course of the day and night, it had descended so inconceivably thick and rapid, as to block up all the roads in such a manner as to preclude the possibility of the mail coaches being able to proceed. One indeed, and only one (from Galway) arrived the next morning. None has ventured to leave Dublin, and it was found impracticable to send the mails on horseback. Thus all intercourse with the interior has been cut off, and it was not until yesterday, when an intense frost suddenly commenced, that the communication was opened. About two o'clock, the inhabitants of this city witnessed the gratifying sight of several mail bags arriving from the country on horseback.

The depths of snow in the streets of Dublin almost exceeds credibility. In many of the narrow streets, after the footways had been in some measure cleared, it was more than six feet. It was nearly impossible for any carriage to force a passage, and few ventured on the hazardous attempt. Many accidents both distressing and fatal, occurred. The distress in that abode of poverty, the *Liberty*,[7] is excessive. In many streets and lanes the wretched inhabitants were literally blocked up in their houses, and in the attempt to go abroad, experienced every kind of misery that it is possible to imagine. It is painful to state, that the number of deaths there have, within the last few days, been greater than at any other period, unless at the time of the plague. We are informed that eighty funerals occurred last Sunday. The coffin-makers in Cook-street can with difficulty complete their numerous orders: and we are pained to state, that not a few poor people have been lying dead in their rooms several days, from the impossibility of procuring assistance to convey them to the Hospital-fields, and the great difficulty and danger of attempting to open the ground, which is very uneven, and where the snow, in some parts, is perhaps 20 feet deep.

---

[7]The Liberty is a Dublin neighborhood that was impoverished in the late eighteenth century. Whitelaw (1805:51–52) reports a "dense population" of 12–16 people per house, a decrease from a few years before, living in "a degree of filth and stench inconceivable, except by such as have visited those scenes of wretchedness."

*Canterbury. Jan. 25.* From the drifted state of the roads, the communication with the metropolis was not open until Saturday, when the snow was cut through by the military at Chatham Hill, and near Gravesend; and the stages proceeded with their passengers which had been detained from Wednesday night. The mail of Thursday night arrived here late on Friday evening, the bags having been conveyed part of the distance upon men's shoulders: the bags of Friday and Saturday night arrived together on Sunday morning about ten o'clock, and yesterday the mail coach reached this city about noon.

*Dalrympte, North Britain, Jan. 29.*—Wednesday, the 26th, was an epoch ever to be remembered by the inhabitants of this village. The thaw of that and the preceding day had opened the Doon, formerly "bound like a rock," to a considerable distance above this; and the melting of the snow on the adjacent hills swelled the river beyond its usual depth, which burst up vast fragments of ice and congealed snow; forcing them forward with irresistible impetuosity, bending trees like willows, carrying down Skelton-bridge, and sweeping all before it. Thus proceeded the overwhelming torrent, in awful majesty, till it had accumulated a most prodigious mass of the frozen element, which, as if in wanton frolic, it heaved out into the fields on both sides, covering acres of ground many feet deep. Alternately loading and discharging in this manner, it called at a door or two in the village, as it were to apprise us of its approach. Impatient of restraint, it deserted its wonted channel, trying to make its grand entry by several courses successively

in Saint Valley, and finding no one of them sufficient
for its reception, it took them altogether, overrunning
the whole holm at once; then appeared here in ter-
rific grandeur, between seven and eight o'clock in the
evening, when the moon, shrinking from so dreadful a
sight, and concealing herself behind a cloud, and the
gloom of night added to the horrors of this tremendous scene. Like a sea, it overflowed all the gardens
on the east side, from the cross to the bridge, and in-
vaded the houses behind by the doors and windows,
lifting and tumbling the furniture, extinguishing the
fires in a moment, and gushing out at the front doors
with incredible rapidity. But its principal inroad was
by the end of a bridge. Here, while the bouses stood
as a bank on either side, it came crashing and roaring
up the street in full career, casting forth, within a few
yards of the Cross, floats of ice-like millstones. By this
time the houses on the west side were in the same situation with those on the east. At one place the water
was running on the house-eaves, at another it was near
the door head, and midway up the street, it stood three
feet and a half above the door. Happily for us it did
not advance five minutes longer in this direction, or the
whole village had been inundated. The consternation
of spectators not unconcerned, may be more easily con-
ceived than described. Several have lost considerably,
and many families have been expelled their own houses,
into which the water is yet pouring, and obliged to seek
shelter from their neighbours. We are still apprehen-

sive of another attack, which, from the present local circumstances, will, in all probability, be worse than the first.

# Accidents

The following are a few of the casualties, which have been the consequences of this severe weather.

The body of a woman was found frozen to death on the Highgate road. She proved to have been a charwoman, returning from Highgate, where she had been at work, to Pancras.

A poor woman, named Wood, while crossing Blackheath from Leigh to the village of Charlton, accompanied by her two children, was unfortunately benighted, and missed her way. After various efforts to extricate herself, she fell into a hole, and was nearly buried in the snow. From this, however, she contrived to escape, and again proceeded; but at length, being completely exhausted, and her children benumbed with cold, she was constrained to sit down on the trunk of a tree, where wrapping her children in her cloak, she endeavoured by loud cries to attract the attention of some passengers. Her shrieks at length were heard by a waggoner, who humanely waded through the snow to her assistance, and taking her children, who seemed in a torpid state, in his arms, conducted her to a public-house; one of her poor infants was found to be completely dead, and the other was recovered with extreme difficulty.

As a party of workmen were clearing away the snow, which was twelve feet deep, at Kipton, on the border of Northamptonshire, a child about three years old was discovered, and immediately afterwards, the mother, as was soon ascertained. The poor woman proved to be the wife of a soldier of the 16th regiment, and she was returning home with her child after accompanying her husband to the place of embarkation. The poor unfortunates, it was supposed, had been a week in the snow.

A respectable, well dressed man was found lying in the road leading from Longford to Upham, frozen to death. The deceased turned out to be a Mr. Apthorne, a grazier, at Coltsworth. He had left Hounslow at dusk on Monday evening, after having drunk rather freely, and proposed to go that night to Marlow. His horse was found in a field on the road side, and had evidently been down. He had property to the amount of 60l. in his pockets, besides a watch and pocket book.

On his return from Wakefield market, Mr. Husband, of Holroyd Hall, was found frozen to death, within little more than an hundred yards of the house of his nephew, with whom he resided.

Mr. Chapman, organist, and master of the central school at Andover, Hants, was frozen to death on Tuesday, near Wallop, in that county.—A young man of the name of Monk, while driving a stagecoach near Ryegate, was thrown off the box on a lump of frozen snow, and killed on the spot.

The Thermometer during this intense frost was as low as 7° and 8° of Fahrenheit, in the neighbourhood of London.

# Chapter I. Frost

> This is the state of man: to day he puts
>     forth
> The tender leaves of hope, to morrow blos-
>     soms;
> And bears his blushing honours thick upon
>     him;
> The third day comes a FROST, *a killing frost:*
> And when he thinks, good easy man, full
>     surely
> His greatness is a ripening, nips his root,
> And then he falls.                    SHAKSPEARE.[8]

Of all known substances, the atmosphere either absorbs or throws out heat with the most remarkable facility: and in one or other of these states, it always is with respect to the surface of the earth, and such bodies as are placed on or near it; for these, properly speaking, have no temperature of their own, but are entirely regulated by that of the atmosphere.—When the air has been for some time absorbing the heat from terrestrial bodies, a frost must be the undoubted consequence, for the same reason that water freezes in a vessel which is placed in a freezing mixture; and were this absorption to continue for a length of time, the whole earth would be converted into a frozen mass. There are, however,

---

[8]From *King Henry VII* 3.2.32–38. *Frostiana* uses the variant spelling "Shakspeare" rather than the more familiar (to modern readers) "Shakespeare."

certain powers in nature, by which this effect is always
prevented; and the most violent frost we can imagine
must always, as it were, defeat its own purposes, and
end in a thaw.


## Freezing

This is the fixing a fluid body into a firm or solid mass
by the action of cold.

A computation of the force of freezing water has
been made by the Florentine Academicians, from the
bursting of a very strong brass globe or shell, by freezing water in it; when, from the known thickness and
tenacity of the metal, it was found that the expansive
power of a spherule of water, only one inch in diameter, was sufficient to overcome a resistance of more than
27,000 pounds, or 13 tons and a half.

Cold also usually tends to make bodies *electric*, which are not so naturally, and to increase the electric properties of such as are so. And it is further found, that
all substances do not transmit cold equally well; but
that the best conductors of electricity, viz. metals, are
likewise the best conductors of cold. It may further
be added, that when the cold has been carried to such
an extremity as to render any body an electric, it then
ceases to conduct the cold as well as before. This is ex-
emplified in the practice of the Laplanders and Siberi-
ans: where, to exclude the extreme cold of the winters
from their habitations the more effectually, and yet to
admit a little light, they cut pieces of ice, which in the
winter time must always be electric in those countries,

and put them into their windows; which they find to be much more effectual in keeping out the cold than any other substance.

Excessive degrees of cold occur naturally in many parts of the globe in the winter season.

Although the thermometer in this country hardly ever descends so low as 0, yet, in the winter of 1780, Mr. Wilson of Glasgow observed, that a thermometer laid on the snow sunk to 25° below 0; and Mr. Derham, in the year 1708, observed in England, that the mercury stood within one-tenth of an inch of its station when plunged into a mixture of snow and salt. At Petersburg, in 1732, the thermometer stood at 28° below 0; and when the French academicians wintered near the polar circle, the thermometer sunk to 33° below 0; and in the Asiatic and American continents, still greater degrees of cold are often observed.

*Wonderful expansion of water in the act of freezing*

Water and some other fluids suddenly dilate and expand in the act of freezing,[9] so as to occupy a greater space in the form of ice than before, in consequence of which it is that ice is specifically lighter than the same fluid, and floats in it. And the degree of expansion of water, in the state of ice, is by some authors computed at about $\frac{1}{10}$ of its volume. Oil, however, is an exception to this property, and quicksilver too, which shrinks and contracts still more after freezing. Mr. Boyle re-

---

[9]This is an exaggeration; there are not many substances, other than water, that expand when they freeze. Most contract.

lates several experiments of vessels made of metal, very
thick and strong;[10] in which, when filled with water,
close stopped, and exposed to the cold, the water being expanded in freezing, and not finding either room
or vent, bursts the vessels. A strong barrel of a gun,
with water in it close stopped and frozen, was rent the
whole length. Huygens,[11] to try the force with which
it expands, filled a cannon with it, whose sides were an
inch thick, and then closed up the mouth and vent, so
that none could escape; the whole being exposed lo a
strong freezing air, the water froze in about 12 hours,
and burst the piece in two places. Mathematicians have
computed the force of the ice upon this occasion; and
they say, that such a force would raise a weight of 27720
pounds.

Major Edw. Williams, of the Royal Artillery, made
many experiments on the force of it, at Quebec, in 1704
and 1785. He filled all sizes of iron bomb-shells with
water, then plugged the fuze-hole close up, and exposed
them to the strong freezing air of the winter in that
climate; sometimes driving in the iron plugs as hard
as possible with a sledge hammer; and yet they were
always thrown out by the sudden expansion of the water
in the act of freezing, like a ball shot by gunpowder,
sometimes to the distance of between 400 and 500 feet,

---

[10]Robert Boyle (1627–1691) describes his experiments with
freezing in *New Experiments and Observations Touching Cold*
(1665). Title XI, "Experiments touching the expansive force of
freezing water" describes the experiments mentioned here. The
full text is reprinted in Hunter and Davis (1999:IV.203–575).

[11]Christiaan Huygens (1629–1695) is well known for his work
on the wave theory of light and other scientific topics.

though they weighed nearly 3 pounds; and when the plugs were screwed in, or furnished with hooks or barbs, to lay hold of the inside of the shell so that they could not possibly be forced out in this case; the shell was always split in two, though the thickness of the metal of the shell was about an inch and three quarters. It is further remarkable, that through the circular crack, round about the shells, where they burst, there stood out a thin film or sheet of ice, like a fin; and in the cases when the plugs were projected by freezing water, there suddenly issued from the fuze-hole a bolt of ice of the same diameter, and stood over it to the height sometimes of 8 inches and a half. And hence we need not be surprised at the effects of ice in destroying the substance of vegetables and trees, and even splitting rocks, when the frost is carried to excess.

# Thames frozen 1715–16

The beauties and usefulness of the Thames, have been almost an endless theme; we shall here describe, how it has contributed at various eras, to the amusement of thousands, when in a *frozen state*. In the frost of 1715–16, this advertisement appeared, "This is to give notice to gentlemen and others, that pass upon the Thames during this frost, that over against Whitehall-stairs, they may have their names printed, fit to paste in any book, to hand down the memory of the season to future ages.

You that walk there, and do design to tell

Your children's children *what* this year be-
fell,

Go *print* your names, and take a *dram* within;

For such a year as *this*, has seldom been."

Dawks's News-letter[12] of 14th of Jan. says, "The Thames seems now a solid rock of ice; and booths for the sale of brandy, wine, ale, and other exhilarating liquors, have been for some time fixed thereon; but now it is in a manner like a town: thousands of people cross it, and with wonder view the mountainous heaps of water, that now lie congealed into ice. On Thursday, a great cook's-shop was erected, and gentlemen went as frequently to dine there, as at any ordinary. Over against Westminster, Whitehall, and Whitefriars, Printing-presses are kept upon the ice, where many persons have their names printed, to transmit the wonders of the season to posterity."

Coaches, waggons, carts, &c. were driven on it, and an enthusiastic preacher, held forth to a motley congregation *on the mighty waters*, with a zeal *fiery* enough to have *thawed himself* through the ice, had it been susceptible of *religious* warmth. This, with other pastimes and diversions, attracted the attention of many of the nobility, and even brought the Prince of Wales, to visit FROST FAIR. On that day, there was an un-

---

[12]Stanley Morrison provides details of this publication in *Ichabod Dawks and his News-letter, with an Account of the Dawks Family of Booksellers and Stationers, 1635–1731* (1931; 2009).

commonly high spring-tide, which overflowed the cellars on the banks of the river, and raised the ice full *fourteen* feet, without interrupting the people from their pursuits. The Protestant Packet,[13] of this period, observes, that the theatres were almost deserted. The News-letter of February 15, announces the dissolution of the ice, and with it the "*baseless fabric*" on which Momus had held his temporary reign; the above paper then proclaims the good fare, and various articles to be seen, and purchased.

> "Thou beauteous River Thames, whose *stand-*
> > *ing* tide
> Equals the glory of thy flowing pride,
> The city, nay the world's transferr'd to thee,
> Fix'd as the land, and richer than the sea.
> The various metals, Nature can produce,
> Or Art improve, for ornament or use,
> From the Earth's deepest bowels brought,
> > are made
> To shine in thee, and carry on thy trade.
> Here Guilleaum, fam'd for making *silver* pass
> Through various forms; and Sparks as fam'd
> > for brass,
> There's T—, 'tween God and *gold* who ne'er
> > stood neuter,
> And trusty Nicholson, who lives by *pewter*,
> Wrote o'er their doors, having affix'd their
> > names,
> *We under-writ*, remov'd are to the Thames.

---

[13]More than one eighteenth-century newspaper went by this name.

There miles together for the common good,
The Slippery Substance offers dainty food.
Here healing *Port* wine, and there *Rhenish*
     flows,
Here Bohea *Tea*, and there *Tobacco grows.*
In one place you may meet good Cheshire
     *cheese*,
Another proffers, whitest Brentford *peas*:
Here is King George's picture, there Queen
     Anne's,
Now nut-brown *ale* in cups, and then in
     canns:
One sells an Oxford *dram* as good as can
     be,
Another offers General Peper's *brandy.*
See! there's the *Mall*, and in that little hut
The best *Geneva*'s sold, and *love* to boot.
See there, a sleek *Venetian* Envoy walks;
See here, an Alderman more proudly stalks.
Behold the *French* Ambassador, that's *he*;
And this the honest Sire, and Captain Leigh.
Here is St. *James*'s Street, yonder the *Strand*:
In this place Bowyer plies; that's Lintot's
     stand."

## Thames frozen 1739–40

The winter of 1739–40, became memorable from its uncommon severity, and the occurrence of one of the most
*intense frosts* that had ever been known in this country,

and which from its piercing cold, and long continuance, has been recorded in our annals by the appellation of the GREAT FROST.

It commenced on *Christmas-day*, and lasted till the *seventeenth* of the following FEBRUARY, when it began to break up, but was not wholly dissipated till near the end of the month. The distress which it occasioned among the poor and labouring classes of London, was extreme: *coals* could hardly be obtained for money, and *water* was equally scarce.

The *watermen* and *fishermen*, with a *peter-boat* in mourning, and the carpenters, bricklayers, &c. with their tools and utensils in mourning, walked through the streets in *large bodies*, imploring relief for their own and families' necessities; and, to the honour of the British character, this was *liberally bestowed*. SUB-SCRIPTIONS *were also made in the different parishes, and great benefactions bestowed by the opulent, through which the calamities of the season were much mitigated.*

A few days after the frost had set in, great damage was done among the *shipping* in the river Thames by a high wind, which broke many vessels from their moorings, and drove them foul of each other, while the large flakes of ice there floated on the stream, overwhelmed various boats and lighters, and sunk several corn and coal vessels. By these accidents many lives were lost; and many others were also destroyed by the intenseness of the cold, both on land and water. *Above Bridge*, the Thames was completely frozen over, and tents and numerous booths were erected on it for selling liquors, &c. to the multitudes that daily flocked thither for curiosity

or diversion. The scene here displayed was very irregular, and had more the appearance of a fair on land,
than of a frail exhibition, the only basis of which was
congealed water.

Various shops were opened for the sale of toys, cut-
lery, and other light articles; even a *printing-press* was
established, and all the common sports of the populace in a wintery season, were carried on with aug-
mented spirit, in despite or forgetfulness of the distress
which reigned on shore. Many of the houses which at
that time stood upon London-Bridge, as well as the
bridge itself, received considerable damage when the
thaw commenced, by the driving of the ice.

The following is an exact copy, of one of the papers
printed upon the Thames, during the memorable frost
of 1740.—The gentleman, whose name appears in it,
(WILLIAM NOBLE, M. A.) had been *one* (of a great
number without doubt) who had their *names* printed
upon the ICE, as a rarity, not likely again to happen.

The original is in the possession of a gentleman of
Whitehaven; but it is not known *who* the Mr. NOBLE
was, whose name and designation it bears.

"The noble Art and mystery of PRINTING,[14] was
first invented by J. FAUST, 1441, and publicly practised by JOHN GOTTENBURGH, a soldier at Mentz, in
High Germany, *anno* 1450.   King HENRY VI. (*anno*
1457) sent two *private* messengers, with fifteen hundred
marks, to procure *one* of the workmen. These prevailed
on FREDERICK CORSELLIS, to leave the Printing-house,

---

[14]This brief history of printing is rather confused.

in disguise; who immediately came over with them, and first instructed the ENGLISH, in this most famous Art, at OXFORD, in the year 1459.

"WILLIAM NOBLE, M. A.

"Amidst the Arts which on the THAMES ap-
  pear,
To tell the wonders of this *icy* year,
PRINTING claims prior place, which at one
  view
Erects a monument of THAT and YOU.


"Printed upon the river THAMES, Jan. 29th, in the thirteenth year of the reign of King GEORGE the IId. Anno Dom. 1740."

# Frost of 1767–68

The beginnings of these years were both distinguished by a very severe *frost*, through which the price of provisions was greatly enhanced. The navigation of the river Thames was stopped, and the river *below Bridge* had all the appearance of a GENERAL WRECK; ships, boats, and small craft, lying in confusion amidst the ice, while others were either driven on shore or sunk by the driving shoals. Many persons perished by the severity of the weather, both on the water and on shore. During the latter frost, the price of butchers' meat grew so exorbitant, that the Hon. Thomas Harley, Lord Mayor, proposed that bounties should be given for bringing fish to Billingsgate market; and this plan having been car-

ried into effect, the distresses of the poor were greatly
alleviated, by the cheap rates at which the markets were
supplied.[15]

## Thames frozen 1788–89

In 1788, a frost began on the twenty-fifth of November,
and lasted seven weeks. On the fifth of January, the
Thermometer stood at eleven degrees below the freezing point, in the very midst of the city. The Thames
was completely frozen over, below London bridge, and
from the variety of booths, &c. erected on the ice it assumed all the appearance of a fair; even puppet shows
and wild beasts were exhibited.

The following diary of remarkable events during this
severe frost, is taken from the Gentleman's Magazine
for 1789.[16]

*Saturday, Jan. 10, 1789.*—Thirteen men brought a
waggon with a ton of coals from Loughborongh, in Le-
icestershire, to Carlton House, as a present to His Royal
Highness the Prince of Wales. As soon as they were
emptied into the cellar, Mr. Weltjie, clerk of the cellars, gave them four guineas, and as soon as the Prince
was informed of it, his Highness sent them 20 guineas,

---

[15]Walford (1887:39) reports that in this year, "the river was
more or less frozen over; but no further attempt at an ice festival
was made."

[16]From *The Gentleman's Magazine* **59**.1:82 (1789); the quotation is not exact.

and ordered them a pot of beer each man. They performed their journey, which is 111 miles, in 11 days, and drew it all the way without any relief.

*Monday 12.*—A young bear was baited on the ice, opposite to Redriff, which drew multitudes together, and fortunately no accident happened to interrupt their sport.

*Tuesday 13.*—The Prince of Wales transmitted £1000 to the Chamberlain for the benefit of the poor, during the severe frost.

*Saturday 17.*—The captain of a vessel lying off Rotherhithe, the better to secure the ship's cables, made an agreement with a publican for fastening a cable to his premises; in consequence, a small anchor was carried on shore and deposited in the cellar, while another cable was fastened round a beam in another part of the house. In the night the ship veered about, and the cables holding fast, carried away the beam and levelled the house with the ground; by which accident five persons asleep in their beds were killed.

In the *common place notes*[17] for February, 1789, it is remarked, 'With the new year, new entertainments commenced, or more properly speaking, old sports were revived in the neighbourhood of London. The river Thames, which at this season usually exhibits a dreary scene of languor and indolence, was this year the stage on which there were all kinds of diversions, bear-baiting, festivals, pigs and sheep roasted, booths, turnabouts, and all the various amusements, of Bartholomew fair multiplied and improved; from Putney-bridge in Mid-

---

[17]In *The Gentleman's Magazine* **59**.1:174–175 (1789).

dlesex, down to Redriff, was one continued scene of merriment and jollity; not a gloomy face to be seen, nor a countenance expressive of want; but all cheerfulness, originating apparently from business and bustle. From this description the reader is not, however, to conclude that all was as it seemed. The miserable inhabitants that dwelt in houses on both sides the river during these thoughtless exhibitions, were many of them experiencing the extreme of misery: destitute of employment, though industrious, they were with families of helpless children, for want of employment, pining for want of bread; and though in no country in the world the rich are more extensively benevolent than in England, yet their benefactions could bear no proportion to the wants of the numerous poor, who could not all partake of the common bounty. It may, however, be truly said, that in no great city or country on the continent of Europe, the poor suffered less from the rigour of the season, than the inhabitants of Great Britain and London.'

Yet, even in London, the distresses of the poor were very great; and though liberal subscriptions were raised for their relief, many perished through want and cold.

On this occasion, the CITY of LONDON SUBSCRIBED FIFTEEN HUNDRED POUNDS TOWARDS SUPPORTING THOSE PERSONS WHO WERE NOT IN THE HABIT OF RECEIVING ALMS.

# Thames frozen 1814

The history of this great frost has already been detailed in our Introduction. We shall now confine ourselves to the events which took place on the marble bosom of the now flowing Thames, from the 30th of January to the 7th of February inclusive.

*Sunday, Jan. 30.*[18]—Immense masses of ice that had floated from the upper parts of the river, in consequence of the thaw on the two preceding days, now blocked up the Thames between Blackfriars' and London Bridge; and afforded every probability of its being frozen over in a day or two. Some venturous persons even now walked on different parts of the ice.

*Monday, Jan. 31.*—This expectation was realized. During the whole of the afternoon, hundreds of people were assembled on Blackfriars' and London Bridges, to see several adventurous men cross and recross the Thames on the Ice; at one time seventy persons were counted walking from Queenhithe to the opposite shore. The frost on Sunday night so united the vast mass as to render it immovable by the tide.

*Tuesday, Feb. 1.*—The floating masses of ice with which we have already stated the Thames to be covered, having been stopped by London Bridge, now assumed the shape of a solid surface over that part of the

---

[18]The original has "Jan. 31," but that must be an error because Sunday and Monday cannot both be Jan. 31; a quick glance at a calendar confirms that the last Sunday of January, 1814, fell on the 30th. This erratum is also noted (by "0" written above "1") in the copy held by the National Oceanic and Atmospheric Administration.

river which extends from Blackfriars' Bridge to some distance below Three Crane Stairs, at the bottom of Queen-street, Cheapside. The watermen taking advantage of this circumstance, placed notices at the end of all the streets leading to the city side of the river, announcing a safe footway over the river, which, as might be expected, attracted immense crowds to witness so novel a scene. Many were induced to venture on the ice, and the example thus afforded, soon led thousands to perambulate the rugged plain, where a variety of amusements were prepared for their entertainment.

Among the more curious of these was the ceremony of roasting a small sheep, which was *toasted*, or rather burnt, over a coal fire, placed in a large iron pan. For a view of this *extraordinary* spectacle, *sixpence* was demanded, and willingly paid. The delicate meat when *done*, was sold at *a shilling a slice*, and termed *Lapland mutton*. Of booths there were a great number, which were ornamented with streamers, flags, and signs, and in which there was a plentiful store of those favourite luxuries, *gin*, *beer*, and *gingerbread*.[19]

Opposite Three Crane Stairs there was a complete and well frequented thoroughfare to Bankside, which was strewed with ashes, and apparently afforded a very safe, although a very rough path. Near Blackfriars' Bridge, however, the path did not appear to be equally safe; for one young man, a plumber, named *Davis*, having imprudently ventured to cross with some lead in

---

[19]The Museum of London exhibited a piece of gingerbread sold—but not eaten—at the 1814 frost fair in 2014 (Anonymous, 2014).

his hands, he sank between two masses of ice, to rise no more. Two young women nearly shared a similar fate, but were happily rescued from their perilous situation by the prompt efforts of two watermen. Many a fair nymph indeed was embraced in the *icy arms* of old Father Thames;—three prim young Quakeresses had a sort of *semi-bathing*, near London Bridge, and when landed on *terra firma*, made the best of their way through the Borough, and amidst the shouts of an admiring populace, to their residence at Newington.

In consequence of the impediments to the current of the river at London Bridge, the tide did not ebb for some days more than one half the usual mark.

*Wednesday, Feb. 2.*—The same sports were repeated, and the Thames presented a complete FROST FAIR. The grand mall or walk was from Blackfriars' Bridge to London Bridge; this was named, '*The City Road,*' and lined on each side with tradesmen of all descriptions. Eight or ten printing presses were erected, and numerous pieces commemorative of the 'great Frost' were *actually printed* on the ice. Some of these frosty typographers displayed considerable taste in their specimens. At one of the presses, an orange-coloured standard was hoisted, with the watch-word ORANGE BOVEN in large characters, and the following papers were issued from it.

"Frost Fair

"Amidst the Arts which on the THAMES appear,
  To tell the wonders of this *icy* year,

PRINTING claims prior place, which at one
view
Erects a monument of THAT and YOU."

Another:

"You that walk here, and do design to tell
Your children's children what this year be-
fell,
Come, buy this print, and it will then be
seen
That such a year as this has seldom been."

Another of these *stainers of paper* addressed the spectators in the following terms: "*Friends, now is your time
to support the Freedom of the Press. Can the press have
greater liberty? Here you find it working in the middle
of the Thames; and if you encourage us by buying our
impressions, we will keep it going in the true spirit of
liberty during the frost.*" One of the articles printed and
sold contained the following lines:

"Behold, the River Thames is frozen o'er,
Which lately ships of mighty burden bore;
Now different arts and pastimes here you
see,
But printing claims the superiority."

Besides the above, the Lord's Prayer, and several
other pieces were issued from these icy printing-offices,
and which were bought with the greatest avidity.

*Thursday, Feb. 3.*—The adventurers were still more
numerous. Swings, bookstalls, dancing in a barge, sutt-
ling-booths, playing at skittles, and almost every ap-
pendage of a Fair on land was now transferred to the

Thames. Thousands of people flocked to behold this singular spectacle, and to partake of the various sports and pastimes. The ice now became like a solid rock of adamant, and presented a truly picturesque appearance. The view of St. Paul's and of the city with the white foreground had a very singular effect;—in many parts, mountains of ice were upheaved, and these fragments bore a strong resemblance to the rude interior of a stone quarry.

*Friday, Feb. 4.*—Every day brought a fresh accession of "pedlars to sell their wares;" and the greatest rubbish of all sorts was raked up and sold at double and treble the original cost. Books and toys labelled 'bought on the Thames,' were seen in profusion. The *watermen* profited exceedingly, for each person paid a toll of 2d. or 3d. before he was admitted to Frost Fair; some douceur[20] also was expected on your return. These men are said to have taken 6l. each in the course of a day.

This afternoon, about five o'clock, three persons, an old man and two lads, having ventured on a piece of ice above London Bridge, it suddenly detached itself from the main body, and was carried by the tide through one of the arches. The persons on the ice, who laid themselves down for safety, were observed by the boatmen at Billingsgate, who, with laudable activity, put off to their assistance, and rescued them from their impending danger. One of them was able to walk, but

---

[20]A tip or bribe (OED, 2018:s.v. "douceur, n.").

the other two were carried, in a state of insensibility to a public-house, where they received every attention their situation required.

Many persons were seen on the ice till late at night, and the effect by *moonlight* was singularly picturesque and beautiful. With a little stretch of imagination, we might have transported ourselves to the frozen climes of the north;—to Lapland, Sweden, or Holland.

*Saturday, Feb. 5.*—The morning of this day augured rather unfavourably for the continuance of FROST FAIR. The wind had shifted to the south, and a light fall of snow took place. The visitors of the Thames, however, were not to be deterred by trifles. Thousands again ventured, and there was still much life and bustle on the frozen element.

The foot-path in the centre of the river was hard and secure, and among the pedestrians we observed four donkies, which trotted a nimble pace, and produced considerable merriment. At every glance, the spectator met with some pleasing novelty. Gaming, in all its branches, threw out different allurements, while honesty was out of the question. Many of the itinerant admirers of the profits gained by *E O Tables*, *Rouge et Noir*, *Te-totum*, wheel of fortune, the garter, &c. were industrious in their avocations, leaving their kind customers without a penny to pay the passage over a plank to the shore. Skittles was played by several parties, and the drinking tents filled by females and their companions, dancing reels to the sound of fiddles, while others sat round large fires, drinking rum, grog, and other spirits. Tea, coffee, and eatables, were provided in ample order, while the passengers were invited to eat by way of recording their visit. Several respectable tradesmen also attended with their wares, selling books, toys, and trinkets of every description.

Towards the evening, the concourse, became thinned; rain fell in some quantity;—MAISTER ICE gave some *loud cracks*, and floated with the printing presses, booths, &c. to the no small dismay of publicans, typographers, &c. In short, this icy palace of Momus, this fairy frost work, was soon to be dissolved, and was doomed to vanish, like the baseless fabric of a vision,— 'but leaving *some wrecks* behind.'

A short time previously to this great event, a gentleman standing by one of the printing presses, and supposed to be a *limb of the law*, handed the following *jeu d'esprit* to its conductor; requesting that it might be printed on the Thames. The prophecy which it contains has been most remarkably fulfilled.

*"To Madam Tabitha Thaw.*
"Dear dissolving dame,
"FATHER FROST and SISTER SNOW have *boneyed*[21] my borders, formed an *idol of ice* upon my bosom, and all the LADS OF LONDON come to make merry: now as you love mischief, treat the multitude with a few CRACKS by a sudden visit, and obtain the prayers of the poor upon both banks. *Given at my own press*, the 5th Feb. 1814.
THOMAS THAMES."

---

[21]Hardened (OED, 2018:s.v. "bony, v.").

It was evident that a *thaw* was rapidly taking place, yet such was the indiscretion and heedlessness of some persons, that one most fatal accident occurred.

Two genteel-looking young men fell victims to their temerity in venturing on the ice above Westminster-bridge, notwithstanding the warnings of the watermen. A large mass on which they stood, and which had been loosened by the flood tide, gave way, and they floated down the stream. As they passed under Westminster-bridge they cried out most piteously for help. They had not gone far before they sat down, but both going too near the edge they overbalanced the mass, and were precipitated into the stream, sinking to rise no more.

This morning also Mr. Lawrence, of the Feathers, in High Timber-street, Queenhithe, erected a booth on the Thames opposite Brook's Wharf, for the accommodation of the curious. At nine at night he left it to the care of two men, taking away all the liquors, except some gin, which he gave them tor their own use:—

*Sunday, Feb 6.*—At two o'clock this morning, the tide began to flow with great rapidity at London-bridge; the thaw assisted the efforts of the tide, and the booth just mentioned was hurried along with the quickness of lightning towards Blackfriars-bridge. There were nine men in it, and in their alarm they neglected the fire and candles, which communicating with the covering, set it in a flame. The men succeeded in getting into a lighter which had broken from its moorings, but it was dashed to pieces against one of the piers of Blackfriars-bridge, on which seven of them got, and were taken off safely; the other two got into a barge while passing Puddle-dock.

On this day, the Thames towards high tide (about 8 p. m.) presented a very tolerable idea of the *Frozen Ocean*;—grand masses of ice floating along, added to the great height of the water, afforded a striking object for contemplation. Thousands of disappointed persons thronged the banks;—and many a 'prentice boy, and servant maid, 'sighed unutterable things' at the sudden and unlooked for destruction of FROST FAIR.

*Monday, Feb. 7.*—Large masses of ice are yet float-ing, and numerous lighters, broken from their moorings, are seen in different parts of the river; many of them complete wrecks. The damage done to the craft and barges is supposed to be very great. From London-bridge to Westminster, Twenty Thousand Pounds will scarcely make good the losses that have been sustained. While we are now writing, (half past 2 p. m.) *a print-ing press has been again set up on a large* ICE-ISLAND, between Blackfriars and Westminster-bridges. At this *new printing-office*, the remainder of a large impression of the *Title-page* of the present work is now actually being printed, so that the purchasers of FROSTIANA, will have this additional advantage.

# Freezing rain, or raining ice

This is a very uncommon kind of shower, which fell in the west of England in December, 1672. This rain, as soon as it touched any thing above ground, as a bough or the like, immediately settled into ice; and, by multiplying and enlarging the icicles, broke all down with its weight. The rain that fell on the snow immediately froze into ice, without sinking in the snow at all. It made an incredible destruction of trees, beyond any thing in all history. "Had it concluded with some gust of wind (says a gentleman on the spot,) it might have been of terrible consequence. I weighed the sprig of an ash tree, of just three quarters of a pound, the ice on which weighed 16 pounds. Some were frighted with the noise in the air; till they discerned it was the clatter of icy boughs, dashed against each other." Dr. Beale[22] observes, that there was no considerable frost observed on the ground during the whole; whence he concludes, that a frost may be very intense and dangerous on the tops of some hills and plains; while in other places, it keeps at two, three, or four feet distance above the ground, rivers, lakes, &c. The frost was followed by a forwardness of flowers and fruits.

# Influence of frost on health

The salutary influence of frosty seasons on the health of mankind is not in the least confirmed by the annual bills of mortality; as many old and debilitated persons,

---

[22]Reverend Dr. John Beale was known for his work in various areas of science. His life and contributions are discussed in two articles by Mayling Stubbs: "John Beale, Philosophical Gardener of Herefordshire: Part I. Prelude to the Royal Society (1608–1663)," *Annals of Science* **39**.5:463–489 (1982) and "Part II. The Improvement of Agriculture and Trade in the Royal Society (1663–1683)," *Annals of Science* **46**.4:323–363 (1989).

whose vital heat is insufficient to excite into action their vessels, already too unsusceptible of irritation, die in consequence of long frosts, during severe winters. Birds, and other wild animals, as well as tender vegetables, perish benumbed from the same cause.

It deserves, however, to be remarked, that a sharp dry frost does not affect the human skin with that sensation of chilly and piercing cold which we experience, when the air is loaded with moisture, the temperature of which is near the freezing point. This remarkable difference arises from the intense degree of cold produced by the evaporation of fluids, which continually takes place on the surface of living bodies, where it naturally produces a more perceptible effect, than the simple contact of *dry* air would occasion, when it is but a few degrees below freezing.

To the young and robust, frost is more pleasing than moist air; as, in the former, they are able to keep themselves warm by increased exercise; which, in the latter, only tends to promote and render the evaporation more severely felt on the skin. For the same reason, severe and continued frosts destroy the children of the poor, who want both food, fire, and clothing in this harsh climate.

In cold countries, the frost frequently proves fatal to mankind, not only producing mortification, but even death itself. The hands of those unfortunate persons, who die in consequence of intense cold, are first seized, till they lose the sense of feeling; next a drowsiness pervades the whole body, which, if indulged in, is attended with imperceptible dissolution.

# Frozen market at St. Petersburgh

To strangers, unaccustomed to the various changes produced in men and things, by the influence of intense
frost, nothing appears more wonderful or noteworthy
than that part of the city dedicated to the sale of frozen
provisions. Your astonished sight is there arrested by a
vast open square, containing the bodies of many thousand animals, piled in pyramidical heaps, on all sides—
cows, sheep, hogs, fowls, butter, eggs, fish, all stiffened
into granite.

The fish are attractively beautiful, possessing the
vividness of their living colour, with the transparent
clearness of wax imitations. The beasts present a far
less pleasing spectacle—most of the larger sort being
skinned, and classed according to their species: groupes
of many hundreds are seen piled upon their hind legs
against one another, as if each were making an effort to
climb over the back of its neighbour. The motionless,
yet apparent animation of their seemingly struggling
attitudes (as if suddenly seized in moving, and petrified
by frost,) gives a horrid life to this dead scene. Had an
enchanter's wand been instantaneously waved over this
sea of animals during their different actions, they could
not have been fixed more decidedly. Their hardness,
too, is so extreme, that the natives chop them up for
the purchasers like wood.

The provisions collected here, are the product of
countries many thousand wersts[23] distant. Siberia, Arch-

---

[23]A werst or verst is approximately 2/3 of a mile (OED,
2018:s.v. "werst, n.").

angel, and still remoter provinces, furnish the merchandize, which, during the frost's severity, is conveyed hither on sledges. In consequence of the multitudes of these commodities, and the short period allowed to the existence of the market, they are cheaper than at any other period of the year; and are, therefore, bought in large quantities to be laid up as a winter stock. When deposited in cellars, they keep for a length of time.

At certain hours, every day, the market, while it lasts, is a fashionable lounge. There you meet all the beauty and gaiety of St. Petersburg, even from the Imperial family down to the Russian merchant's wife. Incredible crowds of sledges, carriages, and pedestrians, throng the place; the different groupes of spectators, purchasers, venders, and commodities, form such an extraordinary spectacle as no other city is known to equal.

# Chronological table of remarkable frosts throughout Europe

A. D.

| | |
|---|---|
| 220, | A frost in Britain lasted 5 months. |
| 250, | The Thames frozen 9 weeks. |
| 291, | Rivers in Britain frozen 6 weeks. |
| 359, | Frost in Scotland for 14 weeks. |
| 508, | Rivers in Britain frozen 2 months. |
| 695, | Thames frozen 6 weeks, and booths built on it. |
| 759, | Frost from Oct. 1, till Feb. 26, 760. |

| | |
|---|---|
| 827, | Frost in England for 9 weeks. |
| 923, | The Thames frozen 13 weeks. |
| 987, | Frost lasted 120 days: began Dec. 22. |
| 998, | The Thames frozen 5 weeks. |
| 1035, | Severe frost on June 24: the corn and fruits destroyed. |
| 1063, | The Thames frozen 14 weeks. |
| 1076, | Frost in England from Nov. till April 1077. |
| 1205, | Frost from Jan. 15, till March 22. |
| 1407, | Frost that lasted 15 weeks. |
| 1434, | From Nov. 24, till Feb. 10, 1435. *Thames frozen down to Gravesend.* |
| 1683, | Frost for 13 weeks. |
| 1708–9, | Severe frost for many weeks. |
| 1739–40, | One for 9 weeks; began Dec. 24. |
| 1742, | Severe frost for many weeks. |
| 1747, | Severe frost in Russia. |
| 1754, | Severe one in England. |
| 1767–68, | Severe frost; navigation of the Thames stopped. |
| 1776, | The same in England. |
| 1788–89, | The Thames frozen below bridge; and booths erected on it. |
| 1791, | Frost and snow in different parts of England, at Midsummer. |
| 1794, | Hard frost of many weeks. Thermometer at London, mostly at 20 below 0 of Fahrenheit. |
| 1796, | Most intense cold on Chrismas-day. |

1813–14   A frost of almost unparalleled sever-
          ity commenced Dec. 27, and broke up
          February 5.

# Chapter II. Snow

Thro' the hushed air the whitening shower
  descends,
At first thin wavering; till, at last, the flakes
Fall broad, and wide, and fast, dimming the
  day,
With a continual SNOW.        THOMSON.[24]


Snow is formed by the freezing of the vapours in the atmosphere. The snow we receive may, properly enough be ascribed to the coldness of the atmosphere through which it falls. When the atmosphere is warm enough to dissolve the snow, before it arrives to us, we call it *rain*; if it preserve itself undissolved, it makes what we call *snow*. It differs from the particles of hoarfrost, in being crystallized, as it were, which they are not. This appears on the examination of a flake of snow by a magnifying glass; when the whole of it will seem composed of fine shining spicula, or points, diverging like rays from a centre.

As the flakes fall down through the atmosphere, they are continually joined by more of these radiated spicula, and thus increase in bulk like the drops of rain or hailstones. Dr. Grew, in a discourse on the nature of

---

[24]From James Thomson, "The Seasons: Winter" (1726); the text of this poem as quoted throughout *Frostiana* does not exactly match that given in the *Eighteenth-Century Poetry Archive*, which is based on the 1735 edition; the first full edition (1730) is a closer match.

snow,[25] observes that many parts of it are of a regular
figure, for the most part, so many little rowels or stars
of six points, and are as perfect and transparent ice as
any we see on a pond. Upon each of these points are
other collateral points, set at the same angles as the
main points themselves: among which there are divers
others irregular, which are chiefly broken points, and
fragments of the regular ones. Others also, by various
winds, seem to have been thawed, and frozen again into
irregular clusters; so that it seems as if the whole body
of snow were an infinite mass of icicles irregularly fig-
ured. That is, a cloud of vapours being gathered into
drops, those drops forthwith descend, and, in their descent, meeting with a freezing air as they pass through
a colder region, each drop is immediately frozen into
an icicle, shooting itself forth into several points; but
these, still continuing their descent, and meeting with
some intermitting gales of warmer air, or in their continual waftage to and fro, touching upon each other,
are a little thawed, blunted, and frozen into clusters, or
entangled so as to fall down in what we call *flakes*.

According to Signior Beccaria,[26] clouds of snow dif-
fer in nothing from clouds of rain, but in the circumstance of cold that freezes them. Both the regular diffu-
sion of snow, and the irregularity of the structure of its
parts (particularly some figures of snow or hail, which
he calls *rosette*, and which fall about Turin,) show the

---

[25]Nehemiah Grew, "Some observations touching the nature of
snow," *Philosophical Transactions* **8**:5193–5196 (1673).

[26]Giovanni Battista Beccaria (1716–1781) was an Italian
physics professor.

clouds of snow to be acted upon by some uniform cause, like electricity. He even endeavours, very particularly, to show in what manner certain configurations of snow are made by the uniform action of electricity. He was confirmed in his reasonings on this subject by observing, that his apparatus never failed to be electrified by snow as well as by rain; and, he adds, that a more intense electricity unites the particles of hail more closely than the more moderate electricity does those of snow.

Snow, although it seems to be soft, is really hard, because it is true ice. It seems soft, because, at the first touch of the finger upon its sharp edges or points, they melt; otherwise they would pierce the finger like so many lancets. The lightness of snow, although it is firm ice, is owing to the excess of its surface, in comparison to the matter contained under it; and thus gold, the most ponderous of all bodies, when beaten into leaves, will ride upon the least breath of air. The whiteness of snow is owing to the small particles into which it is divided; for ice, when pounded, will become equally white.

The beauties of Snow have been abundantly illustrated by poets, both antient and modern; but what can be more minutely circumstantial, or more elegantly accurate, than the following description of Snow from our own admirable poet of the Seasons?

> The keener tempests rise: and, foaming dun
> From all the livid east, or piercing north,
> Thick clouds ascend; in whose capacious
>     womb
> A vapoury deluge lies, to snow congealed.

Heavy they roll their fleecy world along;
And the sky saddens with the gathered storm.
————————————————The cherished fields
Put on their winter robe of purest white.
'Tis brightness all; save where the new snow
    melts
Along the mazy current. Low, the woods
Bow their hoary head; and, ere the languid
    sun
Faint from the West emits his evening ray,
Earth's universal face, deep hid, and chill,
Is one wide dazzling waste, that buries wide
The works of man.[27]

The same author has beautifully described the effects which the inclemency of the season has upon animals, and particularly the feathered tribes, while the snow is upon the ground.

Drooping, the labourer-ox
Stands cover'd o'er with snow, and then de-
    mands
The fruit of all his toil. The fowls of heaven,
Tam'd by the cruel season, croud around
The winnowing store, and claim the little
    boon
Which Providence assigns them. One alone,
The red-breast, sacred to the household gods,
Wisely regardful of the embroiling sky,
In joyless fields and thorny thickets leaves

---

[27]From "The Seasons: Winter."

His shivering mates, and pays to trusted
    Man
His annual visit. Half afraid, he first
Against the window beats; then, brisk, alights
On the warm hearth; then, hopping o'er the
    floor,
Eyes all the smiling family askance,
And pecks, and starts, and wonders where
    he is:
Till more familiar grown, the table-crumbs
Attract his slender feet. The foodless wilds
Pour forth their brown inhabitants.  The
    hare,
Tho' timorous of heart, and hard beset
By death in various form, dark snares, and
    dogs,
And more unpitying Men, the garden seeks,
Urg'd on by fearless Want.  The bleating
    kind
Eye the bleak heaven, and next the glisten-
    ing earth,
With looks of dumb despair; then, sad dis-
    pers'd,
Dig for the wither'd herb thro' heaps of
    snow.[28]

## Uses of snow

We are not to consider snow merely as a curious and
beautiful phenomenon. The great Dispenser of univer-

---

[28]This is the continuation of the previous quotation.

sal bounty has so ordered it, that it is eminently sub-
servient, as well as all the works of creation, to his
benevolent designs. Were we to judge from appearances only, we might imagine, that so far from being
useful to the earth, the cold humidity of snow would
be detrimental to vegetation. But the experience of all
ages asserts the contrary.

Snow, particularly, in those northern regions where
the ground is covered with it for several months, fructi-
fies the earth, by guarding the corn, or other vegetables,
from the intenser cold of the air, and especially from
the cold piercing winds.

It has been a vulgar opinion, very generally received,
that snow fertilizes the lands on which it falls more
than rain, in consequence of the nitrous salts which it
is supposed to acquire by freezing. But it appears from
the experiments of Margraaf, in the year 1751,[29] that
the chemical difference between rain and snow-water
is exceedingly small; and that the latter, however, is
somewhat less nitrous, and contains a somewhat less
proportion of earth, than the former; but neither of
them contain either earth or any kind of salt, in any
quantity, which can be sensibly efficacious in promoting
vegetation. Allowing, therefore, that nitre is a fertilizer
of lands, which many are, upon good grounds, disposed
utterly to deny, yet so very small is the quantity of

---

[29]Andreas Sigismund Marggraf, "Examen chymique de l'eau"
[Chemical examination of water], *Histoire de l'Académie Royale
des Sciences et Belles-Lettres de Berlin* **6**:131–157 (1751). The
spelling "Margraaf" is used in *Frostiana.*

it contained in snow, that it cannot be supposed to promote the vegetation of plants upon which the snow has fallen.

The peculiar agency of snow, as a fertilizer, in preference to rain, may, without recurring to nitrous salts supposed to be contained in it, be rationally ascribed to its furnishing a covering to the roots of vegetables, by which they are guarded from the influence of the atmospherical cold, and the internal heat of the earth is prevented from escaping. And hence, Budinus, in his *Theatrum Naturæ*,[30] observes, that the Psalmist, compares snow to wool, rather on account of the warmth it affords to vegetables in the cold of winter, as woollen garments do to men, than of its fleecy resemblance.

Snow may also fertilize the earth, agreeably to the hypothesis of those who make oil the food of plants, by means of the oily particles which it contains. Besides, snow, in melting, moistens and pulverizes the soil, which had been bound up by the frost; and, as its water has a tendency to putrefaction, it seems, on many accounts, without admitting it to contain any nitre, to be admirably fitted to promote vegetation.

Another reason of the usefulness of snow, has been suggested by Mr. Parkes. Fur and down afford warm clothing, in consequence of the air they infold within them; atmospheric air being a non-conductor of heat. 'Hence it is that the carpet which covers the earth in winter, is spread out by nature with so light a hand, that it might hold an abundance of atmospheric air

---

[30]Jean Bodin, *Universæ naturæ theatrum (Theater of Nature)* (1596).

within its interstices, to preserve the warmth of those innumerable tribes of vegetables which it is destined to protect.'[31]

## Artificial snow

An artificial snow has been made by the following experiment. A tall phial of aqua fortis being placed by the fire till it is warm; and filings of pure silver, a few at a time, being put into it; after a brisk ebullition, the silver will dissolve slowly. The phial being then placed in a cold window, as it cools, the silver particles will shoot into crystals, several of which running together, will form a flake, resembling snow, and descend to the bottom of the phial. While they are descending, they represent perfectly a shower of silver snow, and the flakes will lie one upon another at the bottom, like real snow upon the ground.—In a word, a shower of snow, although so common with us, and therefore so little regarded, is, in itself, a most beautiful spectacle, and is considered by the natives of southern climes, on their arrival here, as the most extraordinary and amazing phenomenon of nature.

## Snow slips

It often happens, that when snow has long been accumulated on the tops and on the sides of mountains, it is

---

[31]From Samuel Parkes, *A Chemical Catechism for the Use of Young People*, which went through several editions in the early nineteenth century.

borne down the precipice, either by means of tempests, or its own melting. At first, when loosened, the volume in motion is but small, but gathers as it continues to roll; and, by the time it has reached the habitable parts of the mountain, is generally grown of enormous bulk. Where-ever it rolls it levels all things in its way, or buries them in unavoidable destruction. Instead of rolling, it sometimes is found to slide along from the top; yet even thus it is generally as fatal as before. Nevertheless, an instance has been cited, sometime since, of a small family in Germany, that lived for above a fortnight beneath one of these snow-slips. Although they were buried, during that whole time, in utter darkness, and under a bed of some hundred feet deep, yet they were luckily taken out alive; the weight of the snow being supported by a beam that kept up the roof; and nourishment being supplied them by the milk of an ass that was buried under the same ruin.

# Account of a woman buried in the snow for eight days

A well-authenticated anecdote of a woman surviving nearly eight days, buried in the snow, without food, occurred near Impington, in Cambridgeshire; and is related by Mr. Okes, the surgeon who attended her, in the annals of medicine for the year 1799.[32]

---

[32]From the *Annals of Medicine* **4**:501–504 (1799), but in that publication, "and is related by..." reads "An account of it has been published by Mr. Okes surgeon, from which we extract the following particulars."

Elizabeth Woodcock, aged 42, of a slender, delicate make, on her return from Cambridge, on the evening of the second of February, being exhausted with running after her horse which had started from her, and becoming numbed in the hands and feet, sat down on the ground. At that time a small quantity of snow had but drifted near her, but it began to accumulate very rapidly; and when Chesterton bells had rung at eight o'clock, she was completely enclosed and penned in by it. To the best of her recollection, she slept very little during the first night.—On the morning of the third, observing before her a circular hole in the snow, about two feet in length and half a foot in diameter, running obliquely upwards, and closed with a thin covering of ice or snow, she broke off a branch of a bush that was close to her, and with it thrust her handkerchief through the hole, as a signal of distress.

In consequence of the external air being admitted, she felt herself very cold. On the second morning of her imprisonment, the hole was again closed up, and continued so till the third day, after which time it remained open. She heard distinctly the ringing of the village bells, noises on the highway, and even the conversation of some gipsies who passed near her, but could not make herself heard. She easily distinguished day and night, and could even read an almanac she took from her pocket. The sensation of hunger ceased almost entirely after the first day.—Thirst was throughout her predominant feeling; and this she had the plentiful means of allaying, by sucking the surrounding snow. She felt no gratification from the use of her snuff. On Friday the eighth, when a thaw took place she felt uncommonly faint and languid; and her clothes were wet quite through by the melted snow. The aperture becoming enlarged, she attempted in vain to disengage herself from her perilous situation.

On Sunday the tenth, a little after mid-day, she was discovered. A piece of biscuit and a small quantity of brandy were given her, from which she found herself greatly recruited; but she was so much exhausted, that, on being lifted into the chaise she fainted.

Mr. Okes saw her that day on her way home: he found her hands and arms sodden, but not very cold, and her pulse did not indicate the great debility which might have been expected: her legs were cold, and her feet in a great measure mortified. She was directed to be put into bed without delay, and to take some weak broth occasionally, but no strong liquors, and not to be brought near the fire. Next day she was affected with symptoms of fever; her pulse was rising, her face was flushed, and her breathing short; occasioned, probably, by having taken too much food, and being incommoded by the crowd of visitors. Her feet were also in a complete state of mortification, her ancles cold and benumbed, and the integuments puffy. Cloths wetted with brandy were applied to her feet, some antifebrile remedies and a little opium were given her. The mortification, however, proceeded, and, on the seventeenth of March, all the toes were removed, and the bones of the heels were bare in many parts; on the seventeenth

of April, the date of the last report, her appetite was
becoming tolerably good, and her health was improv-
ing.

# The hot bath and snow-bath

Almost all the Finnish peasants have a small house
built on purpose for a bath: it consists of only one small
chamber, in the innermost part of which are placed a
number of stones, which are heated by fire till they
become red.  On these stones, thus heated, water is
thrown, until the company within be involved in a thick
cloud of vapour.  In this innermost part, the chamber
is formed into two stories for the accommodation of a
greater number of persons within that small compass;
and it being the nature of heat and vapour to ascend,
the second story is, of course, the hottest.  Men and
women use the bath promiscuously, without any con-
cealment of dress, or being in the least influenced by
any emotions of attachment.  If, however, a stranger
open the door, and come on the bathers by surprise,
the women are not a little startled at his appearance;
for besides his person, he introduces along with him,
by opening the door, a great quantity of light, which
discovers at once to the view their situation, as well as
forms.  Without such an accident they remain, if not
in total darkness, yet in great obscurity, as there is no
other window besides a small hole, nor any light but
what enters in from some chink in the roof the house,
or the crevices between the pieces of wood of which it

is constructed. I often amused myself (says Acerbi[33]) with surprising the bathers in this manner, and I once or twice tried to go in and join the assembly; but the heat was so excessive that I could not breathe, and in the space of a minute at most, I verily believe, must have been suffocated. I sometimes stepped in for a moment, just to leave my thermometer in some proper place, and immediately went out again, where I would remain for a quarter of an hour, or ten minutes, and then enter again, and fetch the instrument to ascertain the degree of heat. My astonishment was so great that I could scarcely believe my senses, when I found that those people remain together, and amuse themselves for the space of half an hour, and sometimes a whole hour, in the same chamber, heated to the 70th or 75th degree of Celsius. The thermometer, in contact with those vapours, became sometimes so hot, that I could scarcely hold it in my hands.

The Finlanders, all the while they are in this hot bath, continue to rub themselves, and lash every part of their bodies with switches formed of twigs of the birch-tree. In ten minutes they become as red as raw flesh, and have altogether a very frightful appearance. In the winter season they frequently go out of the bath, naked as they are, to roll themselves in the snow, when the cold is at even 20 and 30 degrees below zero.[34] They will sometimes come out, still naked, and converse to-

---

[33]From Joseph Acerbi, *Travels through Sweden, Finland and Lapland to the North Cape in the Years 1798 and 1799* (1802), I.297–299.

[34]I speak always of the thermometer of a hundred degrees, by Celsius. *(Note in original.)*

gether, or with any one near them, in the open air. If travellers happen to pass by while the peasants of any hamlet, or little village, are in the bath, and their assistance is needed, they will leave the bath, and assist in yoking and unyoking, and fetching provender for the horses, or in any thing else, without any sort, of covering whatever, while the passenger sits shivering with cold, though wrapped up in a good sound wolf's skin. There is nothing more wonderful than the extremities which man is capable of enduring through the power of habit.

The Finnish peasants pass thus instantaneously from an atmosphere of 70 degrees of heat, to one of 30 degrees of cold, a transition of a hundred degrees, which is the same thing as going out of boiling into freezing water! and what is more astonishing, without the least inconvenience; while other people are very sensibly affected by a variation of but five degrees, and in danger of being afflicted with rheumatism by the most trifling wind that blows. Those peasants assure you, that without the hot vapour baths they could not sustain as they do, during the whole day, their various labours. By the bath, they tell you, their strength is recruited as much as by rest and sleep. The heat of the vapour mollifies to such a degree their skin, that the men easily shave themselves with wretched razors, and without soap. Had *the immortal* SHAKSPEARE known of a people who could thus have pleasure in such quick transition from excessive heat, to the severest cold, his *knowledge* might have been increased, but his *creative fancy* could not have been assisted:—

Oh! who can hold a fire in his hand,
By thinking of the frosly Caucasus?
Or wallow naked in December snow
By thinking on fantastic summer's heat?[35]

# Thomson's description of a man lost in the snow

As thus the snows arise; and foul, and fierce,
All Winter drives along the darken'd air;
In his own loose-revolving fields the swain
Disaster'd stands; sees other hills ascend,
Of unknown joyless brow; and other scenes,
Of horrid prospect, shag the trackless plain:
Nor finds the river, nor the forest, hid
Beneath the formless wild; but wanders on
From hill to dale, still more and more astray;
Impatient flouncing thro' the drifted heaps,
Stung with the thoughts of home; the thoughts
    of home
Rush on his nerves, and call their vigour
    forth
In many a vain attempt. How sinks his soul!
What black despair, what horror fills his
    heart!
When for the dusky spot, which Fancy feign'd
His tufty cottage rising thro' the snow,
He meets the roughness of the middle waste,
Far from the track and blest abode of Man;

---

[35]From *Richard II*, 1.3.295–299.

While round him night resistless closes fast.
And every tempest, howling o'er his head,
Renders the savage wilderness more wild.
Then throng the busy shapes into his mind,
Of cover'd pits, unfathomably deep,
A dire descent! beyond the power of frost,
Of faithless bogs; of precipices huge,
Smooth'd up with snow; and, what is land,
    unknown,
What water of the still-frozen spring,
In the loose marsh or solitary lake,
Where the fresh fountain from the bottom
    boils.
These check his fearful steps; and down he
    sinks
Beneath the shelter of the shapeless drift,
Thinking o'er all the bitterness of death,
Mix'd with the tender anguish Nature shoots
Thro' the wrung bosom of the dying Man,
His wife, his children, and his friends, un-
    seen.
In vain for him th' officious wife prepares
The fire fair-blazing, and the vestment warm;
In vain his little children, peeping out
Into the mingling storm, demand their sire,
With tears of artless innocence. Alas!
Nor wife, not children, more shall he behold,
Nor friends, nor sacred home.  On every
    nerve
The deadly Winter seizes; shuts up sense;
And, o'er his inmost vitals creeping cold,

Lays him along the snows, a stiffen'd corse,
Stretch'd out, and bleaching in the northern
    blast.[36]

---

[36]From "The Seasons: Winter."

# Chapter III. Ice

> The blasted groves their verdant pride re-
> sign,
> And waters, hardened into crystal shine;
> Ev'n the proud Seas forget in tides to roll,
> Beneath the freezing of the northern Pole;
> There waves on waves in solid mountains
> rise,
> And *Alps* of ICE invade the wond'ring skies.
>                                    BROOME.[37]

Ice is a brittle transparent body, formed of some fluid frozen or fixed by cold. (See Chap. I. FROST.) The specific gravity of ice to water is various, according to the nature and circumstances of the water, degree of cold, &c.

The rarefaction of ice is supposed to be owing to the air-bubbles produced in it while freezing: these, being considerably large in proportion to the water frozen, render the ice so much specifically lighter. It is well known that a considerable quantity of air is lodged in the interstices of water, though it has there little or no elastic property, on account of the disunion of its particles; but upon these particles coming closer to-gether, and uniting as the water freezes, light, expan-sive, and elastic air-bubbles are thus generated, and in-crease in bulk as the cold grows stronger, and by their

---

[37]From William Broome, "The forty-third chapter of *Ecclesi-asticus*: A paraphrase" (1727), lines 92–93, 96–99.

elastic force burst to pieces any vessel in which the water is closely contained. But snow-water, or any water
long boiled over the fire, affords an ice more solid, and
with fewer bubbles. Pure water long kept in vacuo and
frozen afterwards there, freezes much sooner, on being
exposed to the same degree of cold, than water un-
purged of its air and set in the open atmosphere. And
the ice made of water thus divested of its air is much
harder, more solid and transparent, and heavier than
common ice.

## Ice-hills

Ice-Hills are a sort of structure or contrivance common
upon the river Neva at Petersburgh, and which afford
a perpetual fund of amusement to the populace. They
are constructed in the following manner: A scaffolding is raised upon the river about 30 feet in height,
with a landing-place on the top, the ascent to which
is by a ladder. From this summit a sloping plain of
boards, about four yards broad and 30 long, descends
to the superficies of the river: it is supported by strong
poles gradually decreasing in height, and its sides are
defended by a parapet of planks. Upon these boards
are laid square masses of ice, about four inches thick,
which being first smoothed with the axe, and laid close
to each other, are then sprinkled with water: by these
means they coalesce, and, adhering to the boards, immediately form an inclined plain of pure ice. From the
bottom of this plain the snow is cleared away for the
length of 200 yards and the breadth of four, upon the

level bed of the river; and the sides of this course, as
well as the sides and top of the scaffolding, are ornamented with firs and pines.

Each person, being provided with a sledge, mounts
the ladder; and having attained the summit, he seats
himself upon his sledge at the upper extremity of the
inclined plain, down which he suffers it to glide with
considerable rapidity, poising it as he goes down; when
the velocity acquired by the descent carries it above 100
yards upon the level ice of the river. At the end of this
course, there is usually a similar ice-hill, nearly parallel to the former, which begins where the other ends;
so that the person immediately mounts again, and in
the same manner glides down the other inclined plain
of ice. This diversion he repeats as often as he pleases.
The boys also are continually employed in skating down
these hills: they glide chiefly upon one skate, as they
are able to poise themselves better upon one leg than
upon two. These ice-hills exhibit a pleasing appearance upon the river, as well from the trees with which
they are ornamented, as from the moving objects which
at particular times of the day are descending without
intermission.

# Icebergs

Icebergs, are large bodies of ice filling the vallies between the high mountains in northern latitudes. Among
the most remarkable are those of the east coast of Spitzbergen. They are seven in number, but at considerable
distances from each other; each fills the vallies for tracts

unknown, in a region totally inaccessible in the internal
parts. The glaciers of Switzerland (see GLACIERS, p.
108,) seem contemptible to these; but present a similar front into some lower valley. The last exhibits over
the sea a front 300 feet high, emulating the emerald in
colour: cataracts of melted snow precipitate down various parts, and black spiring mountains, streaked with
white, bound the sides, and rise crag above crag, as
far as eye can reach in the back ground. At times immense fragments break off, and tumble into ihe water
with a most alarming dashing. In *Phipps's Voyage to
the North Pole*, p. 70,[38] we are told, a piece of this
vivid geeen substance has fallen, and grounded in 24
fathoms water, and spired above the surface 50 feet.
Similar icebergs are frequent in all the Arctic regions;
and to their lapses is owing the solid mountainous ice
which infests those seas.

Frost sports wonderfully with these icebergs, and
gives them majestic as well as other most singular forms.
Masses have been seen assuming the shape of a Gothic
church, with arched windows and doors, and all the rich
drapery of that style, composed of what an Arabian tale
would scarcely dare to relate, of crystal of the richest
sapphirine blue: tables with one or more feet; and often immense flat-roofed temples, like those of Luxor on
the Nile, supported by round transparent columns of
cœrulean hue, float by the astonished spectator.

These icebergs are the creation of ages, and receive
annually additional height by the falling of snows and

---

[38]Constantine John Phipps, *A Voyage towards the North Pole:
Undertaken by His Majesty's Command* (1773).

of rain, which often instantly freezes, and more than re-
pairs the loss occasioned by the influence of the melting
sun.

THOMSON has a magnificent description of these icy
regions:


The Muse
Thence sweeps the howling margin of the
    main;
Where undissolving, from the first of time,
Snows swell on snows amazing to the sky;
And icy mountains high on mountains piled,
Seem to the shivering sailor from afar,
Shapeless and white, an atmosphere of clouds.
Projected huge, and horrid, o'er the surge,
Alps frown on Alps; or rushing hideous down,
As if old Chaos was again returned,
Wide-raid the deep, and shake the solid pole.
Ocean itself no longer can resist
The binding fury; but, in all its rage
Of tempest taken by the boundless frost,
Is many a fathom to the bottom chained,
And bid to roar no more: a bleak expanse,
Shagged o'er with wavy rocks, cheerless, and
    void
Of every life, that from the dreary months
Flies conscious southward. Miserable they!
Who here entangled in the gathering ice
Take their last look of the descending sun;
While, full of death, and fierce with tenfold
    frost,

The long, long night incumbent o'er their
    heads,
Falls horrible. Such was the Briton's[39] fate,
As with *first* prow (what have not Britons
    dared!)
He for the passage sought, attempted since
So much in vain, and seeming to be shut.
By jealous Nature with eternal bars.
In these fell regions, in Arzina caught,
And to the stony deep his idle ship
Immediate sealed, he with his hapless crew,
Each full exerted at his several task,
Froze into statues; to the cordage glued
The sailor, and the pilot to the helm.[40]

# Ice islands

These are composed of a great quantity of ice collected
into one huge solid mass, and floating about upon the
seas near or within the Polar circles. Many of these fluc-
tuating islands are met with on the coasts of Spitzbergen, to the great danger of the shipping employed in the
Greenland fishery. In the midst of those tremendous
masses navigators have been arrested and frozen to
death. In this manner the brave Sir Hugh Willoughby

---

[39]Sir Hugh Willoughby, sent by Queen Elizabeth, to discover
the north-east passage. *(Note in original.)*

[40]From "The Seasons: Winter"; the version in *Frostiana* diverges substantially from the 1735 version but matches the one
published by Henry Wadsworth Longfellow in *Poems of Places:
An Anthology in 31 Volumes*, vol. 20: Russia (1876–79) under
the title "Asiatic Russia: Siberia."

perished with all his crew, in 1553; and in the year 1773, Lord Mulgrave, after every effort which the most finished seaman could make to accomplish the end of his voyage, was caught in the ice, and was near experiencing the same unhappy fate. See the account at large in *Phipps's Voyage to the North Pole.* As there described, the scene, divested of the horror from the eventful expectation of change, was the most beautiful and picturesque.

Two large ships becalmed in a vast bason, surrounded on all sides by islands of various forms: the weather clear; the sun gilding the circumambient ice, which was low, smooth, and even; covered with snow, excepting where the pools of water on part of the surface appeared crystalline with the young ice: the small space of sea they were confined in, perfectly smooth. After fruitless attempts to force a way through the fields of ice, their limits were perpetually contracted by its closing; till at length it beset each vessel till they became immoveably fixed. The smooth extent of surface was soon lost: the pressure of the pieces of ice, by the violence of the swell, caused them to pack; fragment rose upon fragment, till they were in many places higher than the mainyard. The movements of the ships were tremendous and involuntary, in conjunction with the surrounding ice, actuated by the currents. The water shoaled to 14 fathoms. The grounding of the ice or of the ships would have been equally fatal: the force of the ice might have crushed them to atoms, or have lifted them out of the water and overset them, or have left them suspended on the summits of the pieces of ice at a tremendous height, exposed to the fury of the winds, or to the risk of being dashed to pieces by the failure of their frozen dock.

An attempt was made to cut a passage through the ice; after a perseverance worthy of Britons it proved fruitless. The commander, at all times master of himself, directed the boats to be made ready to be hauled over the ice, till they arrived at navigable water (a task alone of seven days), and in them to make their voyage to England. The boats were drawn progressively three whole days. At length a wind sprung up, the ice separated sufficiently to yield to the pressure of the full-sailed ships, which, after labouring against the resisting fields of ice, arrived on the 10th of August in the harbour of Smeeringberg, at the west end of Spitzbergen, between it and Hackluyt's Headland.

# Blink of the ice

The forms assumed by the ice in this chilling climate, are extremely pleasing to even the most incurious eye. The surface of that which is congealed from the sea-water (for we must allow it two origins) is flat and even, hard, opake, resembling white sugar, and incapable of being slid on like the British ice. The greater pieces, or fields, are many leagues in length: the lesser are the meadows of the seals, on which those animals at times frolick by hundreds. The motion of the lesser pieces is as rapid as the currents: the greater, which are some-times 200 leagues long, and 60 or 80 broad, move slowly and majestically; often fix for a time, immoveable by the power of the ocean, and then produce near the horizon that bright white appearance called the *blink*. The approximation of two great fields produces a most singular phenomenon; it forces the lesser (if the term can be applied to pieces of several acres square) out of the water, and adds them to their surface: a second, and often a third succeeds; so that the whole forms an aggregate of a tremendous height. These float in the sea like so many rugged mountains, and are sometimes 500 or 600 yards thick; but the far greater part is concealed beneath the water. These are continually increased in height by the freezing of the spray of the sea, or of the meltings of the snow, which falls on them. Those which remain in this frozen climate receive continual growth; others are gradually wafted by the northern winds into southern latitudes, and melt by degrees by the heat of the sun, till they waste away, or disappear in the boundless element.

The collision of the great fields of ice, in high latitudes; is often attended with a noise that for a time takes away the sense of hearing any thing else; and the lesser with a grinding of unspeakable horror. The water which dashes against the mountainous ice freezes into an infinite variety of forms; and gives the voyager ideal towns, streets, churches, steeples, and every shape which imagination can frame.

# Union of sugar and ice by the agency of fire

In the winter of 1799, (says M. Acerbi[41]) I beheld at Stockholm a spectacle of a very uncommon nature, and such as I never, in all probability, shall see a second time. It was a sugar-house on fire in the suburb, on the south of the city. The accident being announced by the discharge of cannon, all the fire engines were immediately hurried to the aid of the owners. The severity of that winter was so great, that there was not a single spot near, where the water was not frozen to the depth of a yard from the surface. It was necessary to break the ice with hatchets and hammers, and to draw up the water as from a well. Immediately on filling the casks, they were obliged to carry them off with all possible speed, lest the water should be congealed, as in fact about a third part of it was by the time it could be brought to the place where it was wanted. In order to prevent it as much as possible from freezing, they constantly kept stirring it about with a stick; but even this operation had only a partial effect. At last, by the united power of many engines, which launched forth a great mass of water, the fire was got under, after destroying only the roof, the house itself being very little damaged.

It was in the upper stories of the building that the stock of sugar was deposited; there were also many vessels full of treacle, which being broken by the falling-in of the roof, the juice ran down along the sides of the

---

[41]From *Travels through Sweden...*, I.43–44.

walls. The water thrown up to the top of the house. by
the engines, and flowing back on the walls, staircases,
and through the windows, was stopped in its downward
course by the mighty power of the frost. After the fire
was extinguished, the engines continued for some time
to play, and the water they discharged was frozen almost the instant it came in contact with the walls already covered with ice. Thus a house was formed of
the most extraordinary appearance that it is possible
to conceive. It was so curious an object that every body
came to gaze at it as a something wonderful. The whole
building, from top to bottom, was incrustrated with a
thick coat of ice: the doors and windows were closed
up, and in order to gain admission it was necessary
with hammers and hatchets to open a passage; they
were obliged to cut through the ice another staircase,
for the purpose of ascending to the upper stories.

All the rooms, and what remained of the roof, were
embellished by long stalactites of multifarious shapes,
and of a yellowish colour, composed of the treacle and
congealed water. This building, contemplated in the
light of the sun, seemed to bear some analogy to those
diamond castles that are raised by the imaginations of
poets. It remained upwards of two months in the same
state, and was visited by all the curious. The children
in particular had excellent amusement with it, and contributed not a little to the destruction of the enchanted
palace, by searching for the particles of sugar, which
were found in many places incorporated with the ice.

# Glaciers

If any person (says Mr. Coxe[42]) could be conveyed to
such an elevation as to embrace at one view the Alps of
Swisserland, Savoy, and Danphiny, he would behold a
vast chain of mountains, intersected by numerous vallies, and composed of many parallel chains, the highest
occupying the centre, and the others gradually diminishing in proportion to their distance from that centre.
The most elevated or central chain would appear bris-
tled with pointed rocks, and covered, even in summer,
with ice and snow in all parts that are not absolutely
perpendicular. On each side of this chain he would discover deep vallies clothed with verdure, peopled with
numerous villages, and watered by many rivers. In con-
sidering these objects with greater attention, he would
remark that the central chain is composed of elevated
peaks and diverging ridges, whose summits are over-
spread with snow; that the declivities of the peaks and
ridges, excepting those parts that are extremely steep,
are covered with snow and ice; and that the intermediate depths and spaces between them are filled with immense fields of ice, terminating in those cultivated vallies which border the great chain. The branches most
contiguous to the central chain would present the same
phenomena, only in a less degree.

At greater distances no ice would be observed, and
scarcely any snow, but upon some of the most elevated
summits; and the mountains, diminishing in height and

---

[42]From Letter 40 in William Coxe, *Travels in Switzerland: A
Series of Letters to W. Melmoth*, 4th ed. (1801), II.41–44.

ruggedness, would appear covered with herbage, and
gradually sink into hills and plains. In this general
survey the Glaciers may be divided into two sorts: the
first occupying the deep vallies situated in the bosom of
the Alps, and termed by the natives Valley of Ice, but
which I shall distinguish by the name of Lower Glaciers;
the second, which close the summits and sides of the
mountains, I shall call Upper Glaciers.

1. *The Lower Glaciers* are by far the most considerable in extent and depth. Some stretch several
leagues in length: that of des Bois, in particular, is more
than fifteen miles long, and above three in its greatest
breadth. The Lower Glaciers do not, as is generally
imagined, communicate with each other, and but few
of them are parallel to the central chain: they mostly
stretch in a transverse direction, are bordered at the
higher extremity by inaccessible rocks, and on the other
extend into the cultivated vallies. The thickness of the
ice varies in different parts. M. de Saussure[43] found
its general depth in the glacier des Bois from eighty
to a hundred feet, but questions not the information
of those who assert that in some places its thickness
exceed even six hundred feet.

These immense fields of ice usually rest on an inclined plain. Being pushed forward by pressure of their
own weight, and but weakly supported by the rugged
rocks beneath, they are intersected by large transverse
chasms, and present the appearance of walls, pyramids,
and other fantastic shapes, observed at all heights, and
in all situations, wherever the declivity exceeds thirty

---

[43]Horace-Bénédict de Saussure (1740–1799).

or forty degrees. But in those parts where the plain on
which they rest is horizontal, or only gently inclined,
the surface of the ice is nearly uniform; the chasms are
but few and narrow, and the traveller crosses on foot
without much difficulty. The surface of the ice is not
so slippery as that of frozen ponds or rivers: it is rough
and granulated, and is only dangerous to the passenger
in deep descents. It is not transparent, is extremely
porous and full of small bubbles, which seldom exceed
the size of a pea, and consequently is not so compact
as common ice: its perfect resemblance to the congelation of snow impregnated with water, and its opac-
ity, roughness, and in the number and smallness of the
air-bubbles, led M. de Saussure to conceive the following simple and natural theory on the formation of the
Glaciers.

An immense quantity of snow is continually accu-
mulating in the elevated vallies which are inclosed within the Alps, as well from that which falls from the clouds
during nine months in the year, as from the masses
which are incessantly rolling from the steep sides of
the circumjacent mountains. Part of this snow which
is not dissolved during summer, impregnated with rain
and snow-water, is frozen during winter, and forms that
opaque and porous ice of which the Lower Glaciers are
composed. 2. *The Upper Glaciers* may be subdivided
into those which cover the summits, and those which
extend along the sides of the Alps. Those which cover
the summits of the Alps owe their origin to the snow
that falls at all seasons of the year, and which remains
nearly in its original state, being congealed into a hard

substance, and not converted into ice. For although, according to the opinion of some philosophers, the summit of Mont Blanc and of other elevated mountains is, from the glistening of the surface, supposed to be covered with pure ice, yet it appears, both from theory and experience, that it is not ice but snow. For in so elevated and cold a region there cannot be melted a quantity of snow sufficient to impregnate with water the whole mass which remains undissolved. Experience also justifies this reasoning.

M. de Saussure found the top of Mont Blanc only encrusted with ice, which, though of a firm consistence, was yet penetrable with a stick; and on the declivities of the summit he discovered beneath the surface a soft snow without coherence. The substance which clothes the sides of the Alps is neither pure snow like that of the summits, nor ice which forms the Lower Glaciers, but is an assemblage of both. It contains less snow than the summits, because the summer heat has more power to dissolve it, and because, the liquefied snow descending from above, the mass is penetrated with a larger quantity of water. It contains more snow than the Lower Glaciers, because the dissolution of the snow is comparatively less. Hence the ice is even more porous, opaque, and less compact than the ice of the Lower Glaciers, and is of so doubtful a texture as renders it in many parts difficult to decide, whether it may be called ice or frozen snow. In a word, there is a regular gradation from the snow on the summits to the ice of the Lower Glaciers, formed by the intermediate mixture of snow and ice, which becomes more compact and less porous, in proportion as it approaches the Lower Glaciers, until it unites and assimilates with them. And it is evident, that the greater or lesser degree of density is derived from the greater or lesser quantity of water with which the mass is impregnated.

## An icy epitaph

A curious record of an accident, occasioned by the downfal of ice, is to be found as an epitaph, on the son of the then parish clerk, at Bampton in Devonshire, who was killed by an icicle falling upon, and fracturing his skull.

> *In memory of the Clerk's Son.*
>   Bless my i, i, i, i, i, i,
>   Here I lies.
>   In a sad Pickle
>   Kill'd by *Icicle*,
> In the *Year of Anno Domini*, 1776.

## How to make ice

In many countries, the warmth of the climate renders ice not only a desirable, but even a necessary article: hence it becomes an object of some importance to procure it in a cheap and easy manner.—For this purpose, in the East Indies, three or four pits are dug on a large open plain, each of which is about thirty feet square, and two feet deep; the bottoms are covered to the depth of eight or ten inches with dried straw, or the stems of sugar-canes. On this bed are arranged, in rows, a number of unglazed pans made of porous earth, about a quarter of an inch thick, and an inch and a quarter deep, which are filled about sun-set, with water that has been boiled and become cool.—Early in the morning, a coat of ice is found on the pans, which is broken by striking an iron hook into its centre, and then conveyed in baskets to the place of preservation.

The most expeditions method, however, of producing ice, consists in a combination of *sal ammoniac* with *nitre*.[44] It was first discovered by BOERHAAVE,[45] whose experiments were repeated and confirmed by Mr. WAL-KER, apothecary to the Radcliffe Infirmary, Oxford; but he found that his thermometer sunk 32° in a solution of sal ammoniac, when BOERHAAVE's fell only 28°: nitre alone reduced it to 19°. On mixing the two salts, in equal proportions, the power of generating cold was considerably increased; so that the water was cooled to 22°, while the thermometer stood at 47° in the open air. By adding some powder of the same composition, and immersing in the mixture two small phials filled with water, he found it in a short time frozen.

Having observed that *Glauber's salt*,[46] when it retains the water of crystallization, produces cold in a state of solution, Mr. WALKER made an experiment of its effects when mixed with the other salts before men-

---

[44]Sal ammoniac is ammonia ($NH_3$); nitre is potassium nitrate ($KNO_3$). Ammonia is still used in large-scale refrigeration systems today despite its toxicity.

[45]Herman Boerhaave (1668–1738) was a well-known Dutch scientist.

[46]Sodium sulfate decahydrate ($NaSO_4 \cdot 10\,H_2O$) or mirabilite.

tioned; in consequence of which the thermometer sunk
from 69° to 19°, and he obtained ice, while the thermometer stood as high as 70°.—Lastly, by previously
immersing the salts in the water of one mixture, and
then making another of the cooled materials, he was
able to sink the mercury in the thermometer to 64°.
Thus, he froze a mixture of spirit of wine and water, in
the proportion of seven of the latter to one of the former; and, by adding a quantity of the cooled materials
to the mixture in which this was frozen, the quicksilver
fell to the extraordinary depth of 69 degrees.

Various other methods of procuring artificial ice have
been contrived, particularly by the aid of æther; but
that volatile spirit is too expensive for domestic purposes, and a satisfactory account of the process would
exceed our limits.

# How to make ice cream

Ice cream is prepared by mixing three parts of cream
with one part of the juice or jam of raspberries, cur-
rants, &c. The mixture is then well beaten; and, after
being strained through a cloth, is poured into a pewter
mould or vessel, adding a small quantity of lemon-juice.
The mould is now covered, and plunged in a pail about
two thirds full of ice, into which two handfuls of salt
should be previously scattered. The vessel containing
the cream is then briskly agitated for eight or ten minutes, after which it is suffered to stand for a similar

space of time; the agitation is then repeated, and the cream allowed to subside for half an hour, when it is taken out of the mould, and sent to table.

# A palace built of ice

In the year 1740, the Empress Anne of Russia, caused a palace of ice, to be erected upon the banks of Neva. This extraordinary edifice, was fifty-two feet in length, sixteen in breadth, and twenty feet high, and construct-ed of large pieces of ice cut in the manner of freestone. The walls were three feet thick. The several apartments were furnished with tables, chairs, beds, and all kinds of household furniture of ice. In front of this edifice, be-sides pyramids and statues, stood six cannon, carrying balls of six pounds weight, and two mortars, entirely made of ice. As a trial from one of the former, an iron ball, with only a quarter of a pound of powder, was fired off, the ball of which went through a two-inch board, at sixty paces from the mouth of the piece, which re-mained completely uninjured by the explosion. The illumination in this palace, at night, was astonishingly grand.[47]

---

[47]From William Tooke, *View of the Russian Empire during the Reign of Catharine the Second, and to the Close of the Present Century* (1799), I.50.

# Hamburgh ice-boat

The body of this boat[48] consists of wicker-work covered
with leather, to render it impermeable by water; and is
remarkably light, that it may be easily managed by one
person, both on the ice and in the water. Its length,
measured on the outside, is seven and a half feet in the
keel, and twelve feet above from end to end: its breadth,
three feet at the bottom, and four at the upper part.

The bottom of the boat is shod with two small
pieces of iron: and by means of two hooks, the boat
may, with the greatest facility be slided over the ice.
In the lower part or body of the vessel, there is a large
opening, three feet long and fifteen inches wide, the four
sides of which are secured by a frame-work, to prevent
the water from entering the vessel. Through this opening, also, the boatman is enabled to step upon the ice in
those places where it is too uneven to admit the sliding
of the boat, and to carry it, by means of handles.

Another advantage derived from this aperture, in
the middle of the boat, is the counterpoise which a col-
umn of water in its centre produces, and thus prevents
it from being overset, while the man who carried it over
the ice, immediately raises himself above the level of the
water, and sits down in the vessel.

But, in order to approach nearer to the person whose
life is endangered, there is also employed a ladder with
a long jointed handle, which is pushed forward and held
by another assistant standing on the firm ice. On this
ladder the boatman places himself, and advances as

---

[48]See figure 5 on page 118.

near as possible to the body immersed in the water.
Having successfully extracted it, no time should be lost
in laying it in a proper posture in the boat; for which
purpose there is a kind of chair with an elevated back,
on the stern of the boat.

M. Gunther, one of the most active members of the
Hamburgh Society for the encouragement of the arts
and useful trades, informs us in the third volume of
their Transactions, published in 1795,[49] that he has often been present when unfortunate persons have been
rescued from untimely death, by means of the ice-boat,
and that the swiftness and dexterity with which this
machine may be managed by expert assistants, is almost incredible. Hence the vessel is not entrusted to
any other but skilful hands, and during summer it is
deposited in an airy place, and the leather preserved
from becoming either too dry or mouldy. The whole of
this useful apparatus costs only 150 marks currency, or
about 10l. sterling; *a sum so insignificant, that while
the city of Hamburgh has built five such ice-boats, the
great city of London ought to be in possession of at least
an hundred.*

---

[49]Johann Arnold Günther, "Geschichte und ißige Einrich-
tung der hamburgischen Rettungs-Anstalten für im Wasser
verunglückte Menschen" *Verhandlungen und Schriften der Hamburgischen Gesellschaft zur Beförderung der Künste und nüt-
zlichen Gewerbe* **3**:353–438 (1792); the proceedings of 1792 were
published in 1795, which explains *Frostiana*'s use of the latter
year. Günther includes a "mandate concerning too-early skating
on the Alster" describing rules for the supervision of young people that are meant to prevent drownings shortly before skating
season (418–420). His drawings of an ice-boat are shown in figure
5.

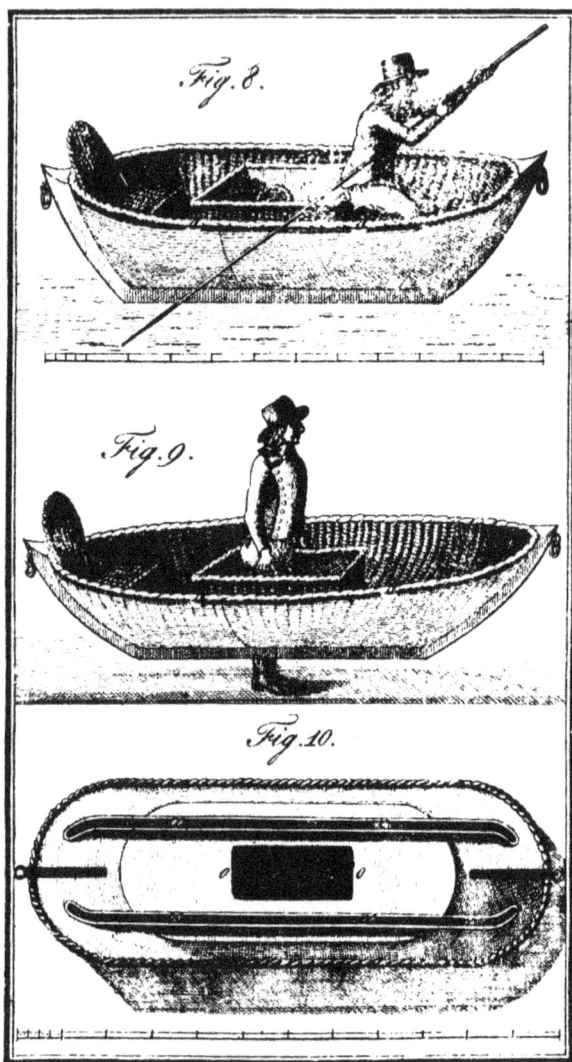

Figure 5: The ice-boat described by Günther. Top: Pushing it along the ice. Middle: Carrying it over uneven areas. Bottom: The bottom. Digitized by Google Books.

# To render assistance to persons in danger of drowning

This desirable object appears attainable by the proper use of a man's hat and pocket handkerchief, (which being all the apparatus necessary) is to be used thus: Spread the handkerchief on the ground, and place a hat, with the brim downwards, on the middle of the handkerchief; and then tie the handkerchief round the hat as you would tie up a bundle, keeping the knots as near the centre of the crown as may be. Now, by seizing the knots in one hand, and keeping the opening of the hat upwards, a person, without knowing how to swim, may, fearlessly, plunge into the water with what may be necessary to save the life of a fellow-creature.

If a person should fall out of a boat, or the boat upset by going foul of a cable, &c. or should he fall off the quays, or indeed fall into any water from which he could not extricate himself, but must wait some little time for assistance had he presence of mind enough to whip off his hat, and hold it by the brim, placing his fingers within-side the crown, and hold it so, (top downwards) he would be able, by this method, to keep his mouth well above water till assistance should reach him. It often happens that danger is descried long before we are involved in the peril, and time enough to prepare the above method; and a courageous person would, in seven instances out of ten, apply to them with success; and travellers, in fording rivers at unknown fords, or where shallows are deceitful might make use of these methods with advantage.

# To recover persons apparently drowned, as recommended by the Humane Society

Let those who first discover an unfortunate object in this situation, remove it to some house near, place it by the fire, and begin by rubbing it with salt, volatiles, &c. and warm flannels, the head a little elevated; never attempting giving any thing by the mouth till signs of recovery strongly appear, and let the person be kept from the crowd of people around him.

The idea that the stomach is full of of water, and thus obviates recovery, is very erroneous and prejudicial, as it is now fully and clearly established, that the respiration being impeded is the sole cause of the suspension of life, and which being restored, the vital functions soon recover their tone; and men are frequently lost from the absurd custom of rolling on casks, lifting the feet over the shoulders, and the head falling on the ground.

# Construction of an ice-house

An ICE-HOUSE, is a repository for the preservation of ice during the summer months.

The situation of an ice-house ought to be towards the south-east, on account of the advantage of the morning sun in expelling the damp air, which is far more prejudicial to it than warmth. The best soil on which such a house can be erected, is a chalk-hill, or declivity, as it will conduct the waste water, without the aid of any artificial drain; but where such land cannot be procured, a loose stony earth, or gravelly soil on a descent, is preferable to any other.

For the construction of an ice-house, a spot should be selected at a convenient distance from the dwelling-house. A cavity is then to be dug in the form of an inverted cone, the bottom being concave, so as to form a reservoir for the reception of waste water. Should the soil render it necessary to construct a drain, it will be advisable to extend it to a considerable length, or, at least, so far as to open at the side of the hill or declivity, or into a well. An air-trap should likewise be formed in the drain, by sinking the latter so much lower in that opening as it is high, and by fixing a partition from the top, for the depth of an inch or two into the water of the drain, by which means the air will be completely excluded from the well. A sufficient number of brick-piers must now be formed in the sides of the ice-house, for the support of a cartwheel, which should be laid with its convex side upwards, for the purpose of receiving the ice; and which ought to be covered with hurdles and straw, to afford a drain for the melted ice.

The sides and dome of the cone should be about nine inches thick, the former being constructed of *steened brick-work*, that is, without mortar, and with the bricks placed at right angles to the face of the work. The vacant space behind ought to be filled up with gravel, or loose stones, in order that the water oozing through the sides may the more easily be conducted into the well. The doors of the ice-house should likewise be so formed as to shut closely; and bundles of straw ought always to be placed before the inner door, for the more effectual exclusion of air.

The ice to be deposited in this building, should be collected during the frost; broken into small pieces; and properly rammed down, in strata of about one foot thick, so that it may become one complete body:—in those seasons when sufficient quantities of ice cannot be procured, snow may be substituted, and preserved in a similar manner.

## Morse-catching on the ice

The Russians who go out to catch the morse[50] are hired for that purpose by a master or ship-owner, who not only furnishes them with the necessary vessels, but fits them out with provisions, stores, and whatever they are likely to want on the voyage, but either agrees to give them a share of what they take, or pays them certain wages. The latter, however, seldom exceed five or ten rubles for the summer; a trifling sum when we consider the hardships, toils, and dangers attending this profession. The morse-catchers usually take with them a year's provisions, as they are often obliged to pass the winter on board their ships. Every vessel has an oven for baking bread and cooking their victuals, for the supply of which they take the needful stock of wood. The only drink they carry out with them is water, with which when they go on shore they prepare

[50]Walrus (OED, 2018:s.v. "morse n.[2]").

quas.[51]—The time of departure varies according to circumstances; some set out at the beginning of summer, when the White-sea is free from ice, others not till autumn, especially if they intend to winter on the voyage. The greatest peril to which they are exposed at sea, is that of being hemmed in by the driving masses of ice; in this case, the ice by its force beats in the sides of the vessel, and the morse-catchers are then reduced to the dreadful alternative either of being buried in the waves on the spot, or of getting on the fields of ice floating at the mercy of the winds, till cold and hunger put an end to their sufferings. And yet it has happened, though very rarely, that some of these poor fellows have been brought alive to land on their flakes of ice.

When the morse-catchers are happily arrived at the place of their destination, the first thing they do is to conduct their vessels to some safe anchorage, where they generally find several little huts that have been constructed by their predecessors in this hazardous warfare, and then commit themselves to the small boats, of which every vessel takes with it one or two to proceed to the conflict with the beasts of the ocean. This is usually done on the first fine day, because then the morses delight in going on the land, or on the ice, to repose; and besides, they are at times stimulated to leave their native element for a length of time for the purpose of copulation, which business lasts with these monsters for a month or two, or to cast their young, or to rescue themselves from the bites of the sea-lice, by which the

---

[51]An alcoholic drink popular in Russia (OED, 2018:s.v. "kvass, n.").

morse in summer is perpetually tormented, and from
which they have no other means of escaping than by
fleeing into an element which deprives these insects of
life. All these causes together collect them frequently
on the beach, or fields of ice, in prodigious numbers.
When the captors discover one of these multitudes, they
must have the precaution to approach them against the
wind, because these animals have so fine a smell, that
they perceive the approach of men with the wind at a
great distance, and then immediately take to the water; whereas in the contrary case they continue lying
undisturbed, though they even see the boat advancing
to them. Besides, the morse-catchers by this means
have the advantage, discovering sooner the place where
this prey has couched; for these fat animals, especially
in summer, emit far round them a horrid stench.

When the captors have reached this formidable en-
campment, they immediately quit their karbasses or
boats, armed with nothing but their pikes, cut off the
way to the sea from the morses, and then pierce those
animals which come first to save themselves in the water. As it is the way with the morses to scramble over
one another in their attempts to escape, from the numbers of the slain there soon arises a bulwark which effectually choakes up the passage to the living; and then
the captors proceed with the slaughter till they have left
not one alive. It sometimes happens that after such an
engagement so great are the heaps of the dead, that the
vessels can only contain the heads or the teeth; and the
people are obliged to leave the fat, or blubber, and the
skins behind.

But, easy as it is for the captors to conquer the morse by land, so dangerous is the conflict with these animals in their own element. We have only to recollect that the morse is commonly of the size of a large ox, and that, besides their sharp teeth, they are provided with two long stout tusks, for judging how a sea fight of this kind is likely to terminate. When any of the morses escape into the water before they can all be killed, the captors leap upon the ice and fall upon the animals with harpoons, which they strive to strike into their breasts or their belly, and to each of which is fastened a long cord. This done, they drive a stake into the ice, wind the other end of the long harpoon-string round it, and are now drawn about, on the piece of ice on which they stand, by the animal till he has lost his strength, when they draw him upon the ice by the cord, and kill him outright.—But when the morses lie so near to the water, that they can leap in ere the attack begins, then the captors fasten the cord, when they have thrown the harpoon, only to the head of the boat, which is then drawn by the huge animal so deep into the water that the sailors must all run immediately astern. The morse having fruitlessly endeavoured to get loose from the cord, rises erect upon the surface of the water and makes a furious attack on his persecutors. In this he is sometimes so successful as to shatter the boat with his tusks, or to throw himself suddenly by a proportionate leap into the midships. Then nothing is left to the crew but to jump overboard and to hold by the gunnel, till other morse-hunters come to their assistance in this desperate situation.—To mitigate the danger of these misfortunes, the captors not only previously take all proper measures, but it is even laid down by laws and regulations what conduct every one is to observe during the voyage and in the actual encounter with the morses. Each of these companies consists generally of a master or pilot, two harpooners, two barrelling people, a steersman, and several rowers, each of whom has his appointed duty.

# Chapter IV. Cold

The Sun

Had first his precept so to move, so shine

As might affect the earth with COLD and
heat

Scarce tolerable, and from the north call

DECREPIT WINTER; from the south to bring

Solstitial summer's heat.         MILTON.[52]

Heat and COLD are *Nature's two hands*, whereby
she chiefly worketh.         BACON.[53]

## Natural history of cold

The properties of *cold* seem to be directly opposite to
those of *heat*: the latter increases the bulk of all bodies; the former contracts them; and, while fire tends
to dissipate their substance, cold condenses them, and
strengthens their mutual cohesion. But, though cold
thus appears, by some of its effects, to be nothing more
than the absence or privation of heat, as darkness is
only the defect of light, yet cold is probably possessed
of another quality, which has induced many to consider
it as a substance of a peculiar nature.

It is well known, that when a continuance of cold has
contracted and condensed bodies to a certain degree, if

---

[52]From John Milton, *Paradise Lost* (1667, 1674), 10.651–656.

[53]From Francis Bacon, *Sylva sylvarum: Or a Natural History
in Ten Centuries* (1627).

then its power be increased, instead of progressively lessening their bulk, it enlarges and expands them, so that extreme cold, like heat, swells the substance into which it enters. Thus fluids sensibly contract in a cold temperature, till the moment they begin to freeze, when they immediately dilate, and occupy more space than they possessed while in a state of fluidity.[54]  Hence, liquor frozen to ice in a close cask, is often known to burst the vessel: when ice is broke on a pond, it swims upon the surface; a certain proof of its being lighter, or of a larger bulk, than an equal quantity of water.

This dilatation of fluids, however, is probably owing to a cause very different from that of excessive cold alone; because the power of freezing may be artificially increased, while the intenseness of the cold receives no considerable addition; and, on the contrary, a substance capable of melting ice, will increase the degree of its coldness. Thus, for instance, sal ammoniac mixed with pounded ice, or snow, melts either of them into water; and increases their cold to a surprising degree, as is obvious from the effects of this mixture, in sinking the thermometer.  Hence the freezing of fluids cannot be entirely considered as the result of cold, but of some unknown property either in the air or water, which thus mixes with the body, and for a time destroys its fluidity.

---

[54]This is true of water, but not of fluids generally; most contract when frozen.

# Effects of cold on the human frame

Its immediate effects on the human body are, contrac-
tion of the cutaneous pores, and a temporary obstruc-
tion of insensible perspiration. Hence we perceive what
is vulgarly called the "goose skin," and the parts thus
affected will not recover their usual elasticity, till the
spasm be removed, either by external or internal heat,
or by friction, which excites the latter.

Beneficent Nature has enabled our frail and compli-
cated frame, to support the heat and cold of different
climates, with equal facility; and though man has de-
vised artificial means of defending his body against the
action of cold, or more properly, of retaining the *inbred*,
or vital heat, yet it often happens that, by exposure to
extreme cold, the fingers, ears, toes, &c. are *frozen*:
thus, the natural heat of those parts is reduced to the
lowest point consistent with life. If, in such cases, artificial heat be too suddenly applied, a mortification will
ensue, and the *frost-bitten* parts spontaneously sepa-
rate. Hence they ought to be thawed, either by rubbing
them with snow, or immersing them in cold water, and
afterwards applying warmth in the most careful and
gradual manner; by which they will soon be restored to
their usual tone and activity.

# Effect of cold on vegetation

Although excessive heat is seldom very injurious to vegetation in this country, yet the defect of that element,
or in common language, excess of cold, is frequently de-

structive to the tender shoots of the ash, and the early blossoms of many fruit-trees, such as apples, pears, apricots, &c.—The *blights* occasioned by frost, generally happen in the spring, when warm sunny days are succeeded by cold nights, as the living power of the plant has then been previously exhausted by the stimulous of heat, and is therefore less capable of being excited into the actions necessary to vegetable life, by the greatly diminished stimulus of a freezing atmosphere.

In the northern climate of Sweden and Russia, where long sunny days succeed the melting of copious snows, the gardeners are obliged to shelter their wall-trees from the meridian sun, in the vernal months; an useful precaution, which preserves them from the violent effects of cold in the succeeding night; and, by preventing them from flowering too early, avoids the danger of the vernal frosts. In a similar manner, the destruction of the more succulent parts of vegetables, such as their early shoots, especially when exposed to frosty nights, can only be counteracted by covering them from the descending dews, or rime, by the coping stones of a wall, or mats of straw.

## Singular effect of cold in Lapland

The effects of these extreme degrees of cold are very surprising. Trees are burst, rocks rent, and rivers and lakes frozen several feet deep: metallic substances blister the skin like red hot iron: the air, when drawn in by breathing, hurts the lungs, and excites a cough; even the effects of fire in a great measure seem to cease;

and it is observed, that, though metals are kept for a considerable time before a strong fire, they will still freeze water when thrown upon them. When the French mathematicians wintered at Tornea in Lapland, the external air, when suddenly admitted into their rooms, converted the moisture of the air into whirs of snow; their breasts seemed to be rent when they breathed it, and the contact of it was intolerable to their bodies; and the spirit of wine, which had not been highly rectified, burst some of their thermometers by the congelation of the aqueous part.

# Extreme cold of Siberia

"Here," says Mr. Gmelin,[55] "we first experienced the truth of what various travellers have related with respect to the extreme cold of Siberia; for, about the middle of December, such severe weather set in, as we were sure had never been known in our time at Petersburgh. The air seemed as if it were frozen, with the appearance of a fog, which did not suffer the smoke to ascend as it issued from the chimnies. Birds fell down out of the air as dead, and froze immediately, unless they were brought into a warm room. Whenever the door was opened, a fog suddenly formed round it. During the day, short as it was, parhelia and haloes round the sun were frequently seen; and in the night

---

[55]Johann Georg Gmelin (1709–1755), a science professor in St. Petersburg, was commanded by Empress Anna Ivanova to lead an expedition through Siberia from 1733 to 1742 (Chang, 2004:104).

mock rooms,[56] and haloes about the moon. Finally,
our thermometer, not subject to the same deception as
the senses, left us no doubt of the excessive cold; for the
quicksilver in it was reduced, on the 5th of January, old
style, to -120° of Fahrenheit's scale, lower than it had
ever been observed in nature."


# Curious effect of cold on the feathered tribe

In February, 1809, a boy in the service of Mr. W. New-
man, miller, at Leybourne, near Malling, went into a
field, called the Forty Acres, and saw a number of Rooks
on the ground, very close together. He made a noise
to drive them away, but they did not appear alarmed;
he threw snow-balls to make them rise, still they remained. Surprised at this apparent indifference, he
went in among, them, and actually picked up twenty-
seven Rooks; and also in several parts of the same field,
ninety Larks, a Pheasant, and a Buzzard Hawk. The
cause of the inactivity of the birds, was a thing of rare
occurrence in this climate; a heavy rain fell on the
Thursday afternoon, which, freezing as it came down,
so completely glazed over the bodies of the birds, that
they were fettered in a coat of ice, and completely de-
prived of the power of motion. Several of the Larks
were dead, having perished from the intenseness of the

---

[56]This probably refers to moondogs or mock moons (parase-
lenae).

cold. The Buzzard Hawk being strong, struggled hard for his liberty, broke his icy fetters, and effected his escape.

## Miscellaneous effects of cold in foreign countries, in former times

The effect of severe cold in other countries, and former times, is thus mentioned by Martin du Bellay,[57] who, affirms, that, in Luxembourg journey, the frost was so sharp, that the ammunition wine, was cut with hatchets, and wedges, and delivered out to the soldiers, by weight, and that they took it away in baskets. Philip de Comines,[58] speaking of the cold, in the principality of Liege, Anno 1769, says, that the wine was dug out from the pipes, out in wedges, and so carried off by gentlemen in hats or baskets. At the mouth of the Lake Mæotis, the frosts are so keen, that on the same spot, where the Lieutenant of Mithridates had fought the enemy dry-foot, and given them a defeat, the summer following, he also obtained over them, a naval victory.

The distress in the retreat of the allied armies from Moscow, can be imagined, if the comparison be made of the miseries the Greeks endured, in retiring from Babylon to their own country. One of which, was, that being encountered in the mountains of Armenia with a storm of snow, they lost all knowledge of the roads, and

---

[57]Martin Du Bellay, Sieur de Langey (1495–1559).

[58]Phillippe de Commines (1447–1511) was long dead by 1769, but his memoirs were translated into English later; *Frostiana* gives the date of one of the later translations.

were a day and night, without eating or drinking, most
of their cattle died, many of themselves were starved,
several struck blind, with the driving of the hail, and
the glitter of the snow. Numbers were maimed in their
fingers and toes, and also became motionless with the
intense cold, although their understanding was not im-
paired. The allied forces had a much longer duration
of similar calamities to sustain and overcome.

# Chapter V. Northern winters

There WINTER armed with terrors here un-
    known
Sits absolute on his unshaken throne;
Piles up his stores amid the frozen waste,
And bids the mountains he has built stand
    fast;
Beckons the legions of his storms away
From happier scenes to make the land a
    prey;
Proclaims the soil a conquest he has won,
And scorns to share it with the distant sun.
                                    COWPER[59]


Before we describe the severity of foreign climes, we
cannot do better than quote the following passage of the
great JOHNSON,[60] which we recommend to the serious
attention of our readers. 'A native of England, pinched
with the frost of December, may lessen his affection for
his own country, by suffering his imagination to wander
in the vales of Asia, and sport among woods that are
always green, and streams that always murmur; but,
if he turns his thoughts towards the polar regions, and
considers the nations to whom a great portion of the
year is darkness, and who are condemned to pass weeks

---

[59]From William Cowper, "Hope" (1782), lines 473–480.

[60]From Samuel Johnson, "Anningait and Adjut; a Greenland history," *The Rambler* (28 December 1751), reprinted at
http://www.johnsonessays.com/the-rambler/no-186-anningait-
and-ajut-a-greenland-history/.

and months amid mountains of snow, he will soon recover his tranquillity; and, while he stirs his fire, or
throws his cloak about him, reflect how much he owes
to Providence, that he is not placed in Greenland or
Siberia.'

# A winter in Stockholm

The snow that begins to fall in the latter weeks of autumn covers and hides the streets for the space of six
months; and renders them more pleasant and convenient than they are in summer or autumn; at which
seasons, partly on account of the pavement, and partly
on account of the dirt, they are often almost impassable. One layer of snow on another, hardened by the
frost, forms a surface more equal and agreeable to walk
on, which is sometimes raised more than a yard above
the stones of the street. You are no longer stunned
by the irksome noise of carriage-wheels; but this is ex-
changed for the tinkling of little bells, with which they
deck their horses before the sledges. The only wheels
now to be seen in Stockholm (says Acerbi[61]) are those
of small carts, employed by menservants of families to
fetch water from the pump in a cask.

This compound of cart and cask always struck me
as a very curious and extraordinary object; insomuch
that I have taken the trouble of following it, in order
to have a nearer view of the whimsical robe in which
the frost had invested it, and particularly of the varie-

---

[61]From *Travels through Sweden..*, I.41–42. Acerbi includes a
drawing of the cart, shown in figure 6.

Figure 6: The cart and cask Acerbi saw in Stockholm.
Digitized by Google Books.

gated and fantastical drapery in which the wheels were covered and adorned. This vehicle, with all its appurtenances, afforded to a native of Italy a very singular spectacle. The horse was wrapped up, as it seemed, in a mantle of white down, which under his breast and belly were fringed with points and tufts of ice. Stalactical ornaments of the same kind, some of them to the length of a foot, were also attached to his nose and mouth. The servant that attended the cart had on a frock, which was encrusted with a solid mass of ice. His eye-brows and hair jingled with icicles, which were formed by the action of the frost on his breath and perspiration. Sometimes the water in the pump was frozen, so that it became necessary to melt it by the injection of a red-hot bar of iron.

Neither men nor women carry any thing on their heads or shoulders, but employ small sledges, which they push on before them. When they come to a declivity, they rest with their left hip and thigh on the sledge, and glide down to the bottom with a velocity, which to a stranger appear both astonishing and frightful, guiding all the while the motion of the sledge with their right foot. The address with which they perform this, it is not easy for any one to conceive who has not witnessed it. If you add to the objects which I have been describing, the curious appearance of the many different pelisses that are worn with the furs on the outside, you will imagine what a striking scene the streets of Stockholm in winter present to a foreigner, especially to one that came from the southern part of Europe.

# Preparations for winter in Russia

On the approach of winter the double windows are put up in all the houses, having the joints and interstices caulked and neatly pasted with the border of the paper with which the room is hung. This precaution not only protects against cold and wind, but secures a free prospect even in the depth of winter, as the panes of glass are thus never incrusted with ice. The outer doors, and frequently the floors under the carpets, are covered with felt. Our stoves, which from their size and construction, consume indeed a great quantity of wood, produce a temperature in the most spacious apartments and public halls, which annihilates all thoughts of winter.

On leaving the room we arm ourselves still more seriously against the severity of the cold. Caps, furs, boots lined with flannel, and a muff, make up the winter dress. It is diverting to see the colossal cases in the antichamber, out of which in a few minutes the most elegant beaux are unfolded. The common Russian cares only about warm wrappers for his legs and feet. Provided with a plain sheep-skin shube,[62] the drivers and itinerant tradesmen frequent the streets all day, with their bare necks and frozen beards. In a frost of five and twenty degrees it is common to see women standing for hours together rincing their linen through holes in the ice of the canals.

The winter increases the necessaries of life, and they are multiplied by luxury. To these belong the winter

---

[62]"A fur gown or great-coat" (OED, 2018:s.v. "shuba, n.").

cloathing, fuel and candles. That people here run into great expences in the article of furs may be well imagined; and the fashion varies so often that a man must be in more than moderate circumstances to be able to follow it. The consumption of wood is enormous. In the kitchens, bagnios, and servants'-rooms, which are heated like bagnios, there is an incredible waste of this prime necessary of life in our climates. Upon a moderate computation here are annually consumed upwards of two hundred thousand fathoms, amounting in specie to about half a million of rubles. This formidable consumption and the rising price of wood, are highly deserving of patriotic attention. The expence in tallow and wax candles is proportionately large. Throughout the long winter we live in an almost everlasting night, as our shortest day is only five hours and a half. In houses conducted on a fashionable style the wax-candles, as in England, are lighted long before dinner.

## Virgil's description of a Scythian winter

Early they stall their flocks and herds; for there
No grass the fields, no leaves the forests wear:
The frozen earth lies bury'd there, below
A hilly heap, sev'n cubits deep in snow;
And all the west allies of stormy Boreas blow.
The Sun, from far, peeps with a sickly face;

Too weak the clouds, and mighty fogs to
   chace;
When up the skies he shoots his rosy head,
Or in the ruddy ocean seeks his bed.
Swift rivers are with sudden ice constrain'd;
And studded wheels are on its back sus-
   tain'd.
An hostry now for waggons, which before
Tall ships of burden on its bosom bore.
The brazen cauldrons with the frost are flaw'd;
The garment, stiff with ice, at hearths is
   thaw'd;
With axes first they cleave the wine, and
   thence,
By weight, the solid portions they dispense.
From locks, uncomb'd, and from the frozen
   beard,
Long isicles depend, and crackling sounds
   are heard.
Mean time, perpetual sleet, and driving snow
Obscure the skies, and hang on herds below:
The starving cattle perish in their stalls,
Huge oxen stand inclos'd in wintry walls
Of snow congeal'd; whole herds are buried
   there
Of mighty stags, and scarce their horns ap-
   pear;
The dext'rous huntsman wounds not there
   a-far,
With shafts or darts, or makes a distant war

With dogs; or pitches toils to stop their
    flight;
But close engages in unequal fight.
And while they strive, in vain, to make their
    way
Through hills of snow, and pitifully bray;
Assaults, with dint of sword, or pointed spears
And homeward, on his back, the joyful bur-
    den bears.
The men to subterranean caves retire;
Secure from cold, and crowd the cheeful fire:
With trunks of elms and oaks, the hearth
    they load
Nor tempt th' inclemency of Heav'n abroad;
Their jovial nights in frolic and in play
They pass, to drive the tedious hours away,
And their cold stomachs with crown'd gob-
    lets cheer,
Of windy cyder, and of barmy beer.
Such are the cold Raphëan race; and such
The savage Scythian, and the German Dutch;
Where skins of beasts the rude barbarians
    wear,
The spoils of foxes and the furry bear.[63]

---

[63]From Virgil, *Georgics*, 3.545–589, in John Dryden, trans.,
*The Works of Virgil Containing His Pastorals, Georgics and
Aeneis: Adorn'd with a Hundred Sculptures* (1697).

# Curious description of a Russian winter in 1603

"The countrey differeth very much from it selfe by reason of the yeare, so that a man woulde maruell to see
the greate alteration and difference betwixte the winter
and summer in Russia. The whole countrey in winter
lyeth vnder snowe (which falleth continually) and is
sometime of a yarde or twoe thicke, but greater to-
wardes the north. The riuers and other waters are
frozen vppe a yearde or more thicke, howe swifte or
broade soeuer they bee. And this continueth commonly
fiue monethes, viz. from the beginning of November,
till towards the ende of March, aboute which time the
snowe beginneth to melte. The sharpnesse whereof, you
may iudge of by this: for that water dropped downe or
caste vppe into the aire, congealeth into yce before it
come to the grounde.

In the extremity of winter, if you holde a pewter
dish or pot in your hand, or any other mettall (excepte
in some chamber where their warme stones be) your
fingers wil friez fast vnto it, & draw off the skin at the
parting: when you passe out of a warme roome into
a colde, you shall senceibly feele your breathe to waxe
starcke, and euen stiffling with the colde as you draw
it in and out.

Diuers not onely that trauell abroade, but in the
very markettes & streetes of their townes, are mon-
strously pinched & killed withall; so that you shall see
many droppe downe in the streetes, many trauellers
brought into the townes sitting deade & stiffe in their

sleds; & yet in summer time you shall see such a new heiw & face of a countrie, the woods so fresh and so sweet, the pastures and meadwes so greene and well growne (and that uppon the suddaid) such variety of flowers, such mealody of birdes (especially of nightingales) that a man shall not lightly truail in a more pleasanter countrey; which fresh and speedy growth of the spring seemeth to proceede from the benefit of the snowe, which all the winter time being spred ouer the whole countrey as a white rose, and keeping it warme from the rigor of the frost, in the spring time, when the weather waxeth warme, and the sunne dissolueth it into water, doeth so throughly drench and soake the ground, being of a sleight and sandy mould, and then shineth so hotly vpon it againe, that it euen forceth the hearbes and plants forth in great plenty and variety, and that in a shorte time. As the winter season in these regions exceedeth in cold, so likewise I may say that the summer inclineth to ouermuch heat, especially in the moneth of Iune, Iuly and August, beeing accounted the three chefest moneths of burning heat, and yet in these places it is much warmer then the summer in England."[64]

---

[64]This is strikingly similar to Giles Fletcher's report "Of the Russe Common Wealth," first published in 1591. The text is reprinted and discussed in Edward A. Bond, ed., *Russia at the Close of the Sixteenth Century* (1856).

# Beautiful description of a winter at Copenhagen

[In a Letter from A. Philips to the Earl of
    Dorset.][65]


From frozen climes, and endless tracks of
    snow,
From streams which northern winds forbids
    to flow,
What present shall the Muse to Dorset bring,
Or how so near the pole attempt to sing?
The hoary winter here conceals from sight
All pleasing objects which to verse invite:
The hills and dales, and the delightful woods,
The flow'ry plains and silver-streaming floods,
By snow disguis'd in bright confusion lie,
And with one dazzling waste fatigue the
    eye.

No gentle-breathing breeze prepares the spring,
No birds within the desert region sing.
The ships unmov'd, the boist'rous winds
    defy,
While rattling chariots o'er the ocean fly.
The vast Leviathan wants room to play
And spent his waters in the face of day.
The starving wolves along the main sea prowl,
And to the moon in icy vallies howl,

---

[65]Ambrose Philips (1671–1749) is known for his pastoral poetry; this poem was published in *The Tatler* in 1709 (Mills,
1870:II.28).

O'er many a shining league the level main
Here spreads itself into a glassy plain;
There solid billows of enormous size,
Alpe of green ice, in wild disorder rise.

And yet but lately have I seen ev'n here
The winter in a lovely dress appear.
Ere yet the clouds let fall the treasur'd snow,
Or winds begun thro' hazy skies to blow,
At ev'ning a keen eastern breeze arose,
And the descending rain unsully'd froze.
Soon as the silent shades of night withdrew,
The ruddy Morn disclos'd at once to view
The face of Nature in a rich disguise,
And brighten'd ev'ry object to my eyes,
For ev'ry shrub and ev'ry blade of glass,
And ev'ry pointed thorn, seem'd wrought
    in glass.
In pearls and rubies rich the hawthorns show,
While thro' the ice the crimson berries glow.
The thick-sprung reeds which wat'ry marshes
    yield
Seem'd polish'd lancets in a hostile field.
The stag in limpid current with surprise
Sees crystal branches on his forehead rise.
The spreading oak, the beech, and tow'ring
    pine,
Glaz'd over, in the freezing ether shine;
The frighted birds the rattling branches shun,
Which wave and glitter in the distant sun.

When, if a sudden gust of wind arise,
The brittle forest into atoms flies,

The crackling wood beneath the tempest
    bends,
And in a spangled show'r the prospect ends;
Or if a southern gale the region warm,
And by degrees unbind the wintry charm,
The traveller a miry country sees,
And journeys sad beneath the drooping trees:
Like some deluded peasant, Merlin leads
Thro' fragrant bow'rs and thro' delicious
    meads,
While here enchanted gardens to him rise,
And airy fabrics there attract his eyes,
His wand'ring feet the magic paths pursue,
And while he thinks the fair illusion true,
The trackless scenes disperse in fluid air,
And woods, and wilds, and thorny ways ap-
    pear;
A tedious road the weary wretch returns,
And as he goes, the transient vision mourns.

# The single night of Spitzbergen

In the dreary regions of Spitzbergen, the Snow exhibits
phenomena not less singular than those of the ice. At
first, it appears small and hard as the finest sand; it
then changes its form to that of a hexagonal shield,
into the shape of needles, crosses, cinquefoils, and stars,
some plain, and some serrated rays. These forms depend upon the disposition of the atmosphere; and in
calm weather, the snow coalesces, and falls in clusters.
    The single night of this dreadful country begins a-

bout the 30th of October: the sun then sets, and never appears till about the 10th of February. A glimmering, indeed, continues some weeks after the setting of the sun: then succeed clouds and thick darkness, broken by the light of the moon, which is as luminous as in England, and, during this long night, shines with unfailing lustre. The cold strengthens with the new year; and the sun is ushered in with an unusual severity of frost. By the middle of March, the cheerful light grows strong; the arctic foxes leave their holes; and the seafowl resort, in great multitudes, to their breeding places. The sun sets no more after the 14th of May; the distinction of day and night is then lost.

> Vast regions dreary, bleak, and bare!
> There on an icy mountain's height,
> Seen only by the Moon's pale light,
> Stern Winter rears his giant form,
> His robe a mist, his voice a storm:
> His frown the shiv'ring nations fly,
> And, hid for half the year, in smoky caverns
>     lie.                                SCOTT.[66]

In the height of summer, the sun has heat enough to melt the tar on the decks of ships; but from August its power declines: it sets fast. After the middle of September, day is hardly distinguishable, and, by the end of October, takes a long farewell of this country: the days now become frozen, and winter reigns triumphant.

---

[66]From John Scott of Amwell, "Ode VII: Written in winter" (1782), lines 10–16.

Earth and soil are denied to the frozen regions of Spitzbergen: at least, the only thing which resembles soil, is the grit worn from the mountains by the power of the winds, or the attrition of cataracts of melted snow: this, indeed, is assisted by the putrefied lichens of the rocks, and the dung of birds, brought down by the same means. The composition of these islands is stone, formed by the sublime hand of omnipotent power; not fritted into segments, transverse or perpendicular, but cast, at once, into one immense and solid mass. A mountain, throughout, is but a single stone, destitute of fissures, except in places cracked by the irresistible power of frost, which often causes lapses, attended by a noise like thunder, and scattering over their bases rude and extensive ruins.

The vallies, or rather glens, of this country, are filled with eternal ice or snow. They are totally inaccessible, and known only by the divided course of the mountains, or where they terminate in the ice-bergs or glaciers we have already described. No streams water their dreary bottoms; and even springs are denied. The mariners are indebted for fresh water solely to the periodical cataracts of melted snow in the short season of summer, or to pools in the middle of the vast fields of ice.

Yet, even here, Flora deigns to make a short visit, and to scatter a scanty stock over the bases of the hills: her efforts never rise beyond a few humble herbs, which shoot, flower, and seed, in the short warmth of June and July, and then wither into rest until the succeed-

ing year. Among these, however, the salubrious scurvy-
grass, the resource of distempered frames, is providen-
tially most abundant.

Such, after all, is the aspsect of extreme sterlity and
desolation in these dreary regions, that we can scarcely
imagine any mortal would be so hardy as to make them
even a temporary abode. Yet here did four Russian
mariners, who were accidentally left on this frozen coast
in the year 1743, live six years (one excepted), till happily released by the arrival of a ship. In 1633, seven
Dutch sailors were voluntarily left here to pass the winter, and to make their remarks; but they all perished
from the effects of the scurvy. In the following year,
seven more self-devoted victims of the same nation un-
derwent a similar fate: yet all these adventurous men
had been liberally provided with medicines, and every
necessary for the preservation of life. Eight English-
men, left by accident in the same country, in 1650, were
far more forunate: unprovided with every thing, they
contrived, however, to frame a hut of some old materials, and were found by the returning ships, the next
year, in perfect health. The Russians, have lately attempted to colonize these dreadful islands. They have
annually sent parties to continue there the whole year,
who have established settlements at Spitzbergen and
other places adjacent, where they have built huts, each
of which is occupied by two boats' crews, or twenty-
six men. They bring with them salted fish, rye-flour,
and the serum or whey of sour milk. The whey is their
chief beverage, and is also used in baking their bread.
Each hut has an oven which serves also as a stove; and

their fuel is wood, which they bring with them from Archangel. Their huts are above ground, and surprisingly warm. They boil their fish with water and rye-meal: this is their winter diet. In summer, they live chiefly on fowls, or their eggs. They are dressed in the skins of the bear or the reindeer, with the fur side next their bodies; their bedding, likewise, is formed of the same. The skin of the fox, which is the most valuable, is preserved as an article of commerce. They have also other employment beside the chase, in catching, with nets, the beluga, or white whale. Few of them die from the severity of the cold; but they are often frost-bitten, so as to lose their toes or fingers; for they are so hardy as to hunt in all weathers. They are at liberty to leave the place by the 22d of September, whether they are relieved by a fresh party from Russia, or not. The great exercise they use; their vegetable food; their method of freshening their salt provision, by boiling it in water, and mixing it with flour; their beverage of whey; and their total abstinence from spirituous liquors; are the happy preservatives from the scurvy, which brought all the preceding adventurers, who perished, to their miserable end.

# Sledges

As sledges are much used in these northern countries, we shall briefly describe those used in Holland, Lapland, and Kamschatka.

These carriages are *without wheels*, and are frequently appropriated for carrying large weights, as huge stones,

bells, etc. etc. The sledge on which a criminal is taken
to the place of execution, is called a *hurdle.* But in
cold countries, sledges are substituted for wheel carriages, being more convenient for travelling on the *ice,*
and over the boundless *snows.*

*Dutch sledges*

By the polite laws of Amsterdam, wheel-carriages are
limited to a certain number, which is very inconsider-
able compared with the size of the city, from an apprehension that an uncontrolled use of them might hazard
the foundation of the houses, most of which are built
upon piles; for nearly the whole of the ground on which
this vast city stands was formerly a morass. A carriage, called by the Dutch a sley, and by the French
a *traineau,* is used in their room; it is the body of a
coach fastened by ropes on a sledge, and drawn by one
horse; the driver walks by the side of it, which he holds
with one hand to prevent its falling over, and with the
other the reins. Nothing can be more melancholy than
this machine, which holds four persons, moves at the
rate of about three miles an hour, and seems more like
the equipage of an hospital, than a vehicle in which the
observer would expect to find a merry face; yet in this
manner do the Dutch frequently pay visits and take the
air.

*Dogs* are frequently employed in Holland, to draw
*light sledges* tilted for the conveyance of provisions, etc.
to a short distance. In Holland, according to Mr. Pratt,
there is not an idle dog, of any material size, to be seen
in the whole seven provinces. You see them in *harness,*

at all parts of the Hague, as well as in other towns, tug-
ging at sledges or little carts with their tongue nearly
sweeping the ground, and their poor palpitating hearts
almost beating through their sides: frequently, three,
four, five, or sometimes six abreast, drawing *men* and
*merchandize* with the speed of little horses. On passing from Hague gate to Scheveling, you perceive at any
hour of the day, an incredible number *loaded with fish
and men*, under the burthen of which they run off at a
long trot, and sometimes at full gallop, *the whole mile
and half*, which is the precise distance from gate to gate;
nor on their return are they suffered to come with their
sledges empty, being filled not only with the men and
boys before mentioned, but with such commodities as
are marketable at the village. This writer further adds,
that it is no uncommon thing in the middle of summer,
to see these poor, patient, persevering animals urged
and driven, beyond their utmost ability, till they drop
down on the road.[67]


*Ship-sledges*

The Dutch have also a kind of sledge, on which they
*can carry a vessel* of any burthen *by land*. It consists of
a plank of the length of a keel of a moderate ship raised
a little behind, and hollow in the middle; so that the
sides go a little a slope, and are furnished with holes to
receive pins, etc. The rest is quite even.

---

[67]From Samuel Jackson Pratt, *Gleanings through Wales, Holland, and Westphalia: with Views of Peace and War at Home
and Abroad* (1795), II.67–68, with some emendations.

*Lapland sledges*

These carriages are extremely light and elegant, and are
covered at the bottom with the skin of the rein-deer.
They are yoked to the sledge by a collar, from which a
trace is brought under the belly, between the legs, and
fastened to the forepart of the machine. The person
who sits in it guides the animal with a cord fastened
to its horns; he drives it with a goad, and encourages
it with his voice. Those of the wild breed, though by
far the strongest, often prove refractory, and not only
refuse to obey their masters, but turn against him and
strike so furiously with their feet, that his only resource
is to cover himself with his sledge, upon which the en-
raged creature vents his fury: the tame deer on the
contrary, is patient, active, and willing. When hard
pushed, the rein deer will trot the distance of *sixty
miles without stopping;* but, in such exertions, the poor,
obedient creature fatigues itself so exceedingly, that its
master is frequently obliged to kill it immediately, to
prevent a lingering death that would ensue. In general,
they can go *thirty miles* without stopping, and that
without any great or dangerous effort.

> Obsequious at their call, the docile tribe
> Yield to the *sled* their necks, and whirl them
>     swift
> O'er hill and dale, heaped into one expanse
> Of *marbled snow*, as far as eye can sweep,
> *With a blue crust of ice unbounded glazed.*[68]

---

[68]From "The Seasons: Winter"; this passage is not in the 1735
version but is in the 1730 version.

*Sledges in Kamschatka*

The only method of travelling in this dreary country, during the winter is, drawn on a sledge by the strong, nimble, and active dogs of the country. They travel with great expedition. Capt. King[69] relates, that during his stay there, a courier with dispatches, drawn by them, performed a journey of *two hundred and seventy* miles in *less than four days*.

The sledges are usually drawn by *five dogs*, four of them yoked two and two abreast: the foremost acts as a leader to the rest. The reins being fastened to a collar round the leading dog's neck, are of little use in directing the pack; the driver depending chiefly on their obedience to his voice, with which he animates them to proceed. Great care and attention are consequently used in training up those for leaders, which are more valuable according to their steadiness and docility; the sum of forty roubles, or nine pounds being no unusual price for them. The rider has a crooked stick, answering the purpose of both whip and reins; with which, by striking on the snow, he regulates the speed of the dogs, or stops them at his pleasure. When they are inattentive to their duty, he often chastises them by throwing it at them. He discovers great dexterity in regaining his stick, which is the greatest difficulty attending his situation; for if he should happen to lose it, the dogs immediately discover the circumstance, and never fail

---

[69]Captain James King (1750–1784) is known for his exploratory voyages, including one to the Kamchatka Peninsula in eastern Russia. His description is published in *A Voyage to the Pacific Ocean* (1785).

to set off at full speed, and continue to run till their
strength is exhausted, or till the carriage is overturned,
and dashed to pieces, or hurried down a precipice.

# Chapter VI. Skating

In giddy circles, whirling variously,
The *skater* fleetly thrids the mazy throng.
Trust not *incautiously* the smooth expanse;
For oft a treach'rous thaw, ere yet perceived,
Saps, by degrees, the solid-seeming mass.[70]


The winter of England, usually allows but few of those pastimes which continue for so long a period, in more northerly regions.


On blithsome frolicks bent, the youthful swains,
While every work of man is laid at rest,
Fond o'er the river crowd in various sports
And revelry dissolved; where mixing glad,
Happiest of all the train! the raptured boy
Lashes the whirling top. Or, where the *Rhine*
Branches out in many a long canal extends,
From every province swarming, void of care,
*Batavia* rushes forth; and as *they sweep,*
*On sounding Skates, a thousand different*
    *ways*
*Or circling poise, swift as the wind, along,*
The then gay land is maddened all to joy.
Nor less the Northern Courts, wide o'er the
    snow
Pour a new pomp. Eager, on rapid sleds

---

[70]From James Grahame, "February" in *The Rural Calendar* (1797), lines 12–13, 19–21.

Their vig'rous youth in bold contention wheel
The long resounding course. Mean-time, to
    raise
The manly strife, with highly-blooming charms,
Flushed by the season, Scandinavia's dames,
Or Russia's buxom daughters, glow around.[71]


Much of the above description, however, has for these few weeks past been realised, by the busy crowds assembled on our principal rivers and reservoirs. The Canal in St. James's Park, the Serpentine, and the noble THAMES Rivers, still daily present to our observation a truly delightful spectacle—a complete FROST FAIR, to which the pencil of a TENIERS,[72] or a WILKIE,[73] could alone do justice. The compiler of this work has been highly gratified with seeing the number of young persons engaged in the active and healthful employment of SKATING; and from a view to their improvement in this useful and elegant art, he has collected together some valuable information on the subject,— which he offers to the notice of his young friends, accompanied by his best wishes for the success of his instructions. These, if attended to, cannot fail of making an elegant and fearless Skater.

---

[71] From "The Seasons: Winter"; this passage diverges considerably from the 1735 version but reflects the 1730 version accurately.

[72] There were four Flemish painters called "David Teniers" in the sixteenth through eighteenth centuries.

[73] Sir David Wilkie (1785–1841), a well-known painter from Scotland.

# Origin of skating

Although the ancients were remarkable for for their dexterity in most of the athletic sports, yet skating seems to have been unknown to them. According to the antiquaries, this exercise made its appearance in the thirteenth century.[74],[75] It probably derived its origin in Holland, where it was practised, not only as a graceful and elegant amusement, but as an expeditious mode of travelling when the lakes and canals were frozen up during winter. In Holland, long journies are made upon skates with ease and expedition; but in general, less attention is there paid to graceful and elegant movements, than to the expedition and celerity of what is called *journey skating.* It is only in those countries where it is considered as an amusement that its graceful attitudes and movements can be studied; and there is no exercise whatever better calculated to set off the human figure to advantage.

The acquirement of most exercises may be attained at an advanced period of life; but to become an expert skater, it is necessary to begin the practice of the art at a very early age. It is difficult to reduce the art of

---

[74]As to *sliding* it is much older; and, although we cannot fix the precise date, we suppose that *sliding* and *ice* came in together. The slips, however, and trips made in our days, are, perhaps, real improvements; they have *great variety,* and we question if it may not be said that *every man invents his own downfal. (Note in original.)*

[75]This is about right. The evidence for ice skates made from animal bones goes back to about 2500 BC, but the earliest metal-bladed skates found to date are from the early thirteenth century. See Küchelmann and Zidarov (2005) for more information.

skating to a system.[76] It is principally by the imitation
of a good skater that a young beginner can form his
own practice. The English, though often remarkable
for feats of agility upon skates, are very deficient in
gracefulness; which is partly owing to the construction
of the skates. They are too much curved in the surface
which embraces the ice, consequently they involuntarily
bring the users of them round on the outside upon a
quick and small circle; whereas the skater, by using
skates of a different construction, less curved, has the
command of his stroke, and can enlarge or diminish the
circle according to his own wish or desire.

## Rules for learners

Those who wish to be proficients should begin at an
early period of life; and should first endeavour to throw
off the fear which always attends the commencement of
an apparently hazardous amusement. They will soon
acquire a facility of moving on the *inside*: when they
have done this, they must endeavour to acquire the
movement on the *outside* of the skates; which is nothing
more than throwing themselves upon the *outer edge* of
the skate, and making the balance of their body tend
towards that side, which will necessarily enable them
to form a semicircle. In this, much assistance may be
derived from placing a *bag of lead-shot* in the pocket

---

[76]Despite this difficulty, figure skating was reduced to a system
by Henry Eugene Vandervell and T. Maxwell Witham just over
half a century after the publication of *Frostiana* (Vandervell and
Witham, 1869).

next to the *foot employed in making the outside stroke*, which will produce an artificial poise of the body; this afterwards will become natural by practice.

At the commencement of the outside stroke, the knee of the employed limb should be a little bent, and gradually brought to a rectilineal position when the stroke is completed.—The following rules should also be carefully practised and strictly attended to:—they will be of the greatest service.

1. When the practitioner becomes expert in forming the semicircle with both feet, he is then to join them together, and proceed progressively and alternately with both feet, which will carry him forward with a graceful movement.

2. Care should be taken to use very little muscular exertion, for the impelling motion should proceed from the mechanical impulse of the body thrown into such a position as to regulate the stroke.

3. At taking the outside stroke, the body ought to be thrown forward easily, the unemployed limb kept in a direct line with the body, and the face and eyes directly looking forward: the unemployed foot ought to be stretched towards the ice, with the toes in a direct line with the leg.

4. In the time of making the curve, the body must be gradually, and almost imperceptibly, raised, and the unemployed limb brought in the same manner forward: so that, at finishing the curve, the body will bend a small degree backward, and the unemployed foot will be about two inches before the other, ready to embrace the ice and form a correspondent curve.

5. The muscular movement of the whole body must correspond with the movement of the skate, and should be regulated so as to be almost imperceptible to the spectators.

6. Particular attention should be paid in carrying round the head and eyes with a regular and imperceptible motion; for nothing so much diminishes the grace and elegance of skating as sudden jerks, and exertions, which are so frequently used by the generality of skaters.

7. The management of the arms likewise deserves attention. There is no mode of disposing of them more gracefully in skating outside, than folding the hands into each other, or using a muff.

There are various feats of activity and manœuvres used upon skates; but they are so various that we cannot pretend to detail them. *Moving on the outside* is the primary object for a skater to attain; and when he becomes an adept in that, he will easily acquire a facility in executing other branches of the art. There are few exercises but will afford him hints of elegant and graceful attitudes. For example, nothing can be more beautiful than the attitude of *drawing the bow and arrow* while the skater is making a large circle on the outside: the *manual exercise* and *military salutes* have likewise a pretty effect when used by an expert skater.

Skating is an amusement, well calculated for the severity of winter; as it contributes to promote both insensible perspiration, and the circulation of the blood. Hence, a Society has even been, formed in Edinburgh,

under the name of the *Skating-club*;[77] the avowed object of which is the improvement of this recreation, so
as to reduce it to the rules of art.—Excellence, however, can be attained only by observing the motions
of a skilful skater. This innocent pursuit, especially in
the South of Britain, where the winters are generally
mild, should not be encouraged, unless the ice be of
considerable thickness: at the same time, some precaution is necessary to retire from this enticing diversion
in *proper* time; because the body, being thrown into
*sensible* perspiration, is thus rendered more susceptible of cold; and, unless due attention be paid to this
circumstance, a cold will probably be the consequence.

We have heard that some skaters in the fens of
Cambridgeshire and Huntingdonshire, have skated *two
miles* in TWO MINUTES, the strokes on an average being each ten yards. This velocity exceeds that of most
race horses, and the fatigue occasioned by it is much
less.[78]

A very remarkable skating-feat is said to have taken

---

[77]The Edinburgh Skating Club was probably founded in the
1760s; it is best remembered for its admission test: skaters seek-
ing to join were required "to skate a complete circle on either foot,
and jump over first one, then two, then three hats" (Thurber,
2018:55–56, 98).

[78]This seems exaggerated; these skaters supposedly averaged
60 miles per hour. In December 2017, Ted-Jan Bloemen of
Canada set a world record of 6:01.86 in the men's 5000 meter-
speed skating event (International Skating Union, 2017), which
is equivalent to an average velocity of approximately 31 miles
per hour, only half as fast as these supposed nineteenth-century
skaters despite substantial advances in skate technology. On 31
March 2018, *The Local* reported that Dutch speed skater Kjeld

place during the late frost. A Mr. Maxwell, celebrated for his skill and dexterity in this useful art, *skated from Long Acre to St. James's Park* in FOUR MINUTES and *fifty seconds.* This was for a wager, and the given time was FIVE MINUTES.

To the native of HOLLAND, skating is quite as familiar as walking, and he puts on his skates with the same indifference as we do our shoes;—these instruments, indeed, are indispensable to the Dutch in the winter season; and are used by men, WOMEN, and *children*, constantly. The women skate to market with provisions, and *children of five or six years old* and upwards, accompany them, not lazily hanging at their backs or on their arms, but each little skater with *winged feet* flies after its mother, and carries a little basket of eggs, or other articles along with it. *Interesting scene!* How admirably adapted are the manners and customs of mankind to the climates appointed for them by Providence. Skating is pursued in England as an *amusement only*, and for a single week, perhaps, in the course of the year; but in *Holland*, it is absolutely *necessary*, and supplies a cheap and commodious method of transport to all classes of people.

The Dutch skates are not so finely shaped as those we use; and the *skaters* are more remarkable for the *ease*, than *elegance* of their execution.

---

Nuis reached 93 kilometers per hour (approximately 58 miles per hour) on skates by following a car dragging an aerodynamic shield to reduce wind resistance (Anonymous, 2018).

*This day is published by* SHERWOOD *and Co.*
*price 9s. boards, (second edition)*

TIME'S TELESCOPE for 1814; or a Complete Guide
to the Almanack: containing an Explanation of Saints'
Days, Astronomical Occurrences, and Naturalist's Diary, for every Month in the Year; with Twelve descrip-
tive Wood-cuts by Mr. Clennell.[79]

---

[79]This advertisement appeared at the end of *Frostiana* and is
left here for completeness despite its irrelevance. The January
section of the advertised book has some overlap with *Frostiana*.

www.ingramcontent.com/pod-product-compliance
Lightning Source LLC
Chambersburg PA
CBHW031125020426
42333CB00012B/243